THE
THERAPY
of POETRY

THE
THERAPY
of POETRY

By
Molly Harrower, Ph.D., D.H.L.
Professor Emeritus
Dept. of Health & Clinical Psychology
University of Florida
Gainesville, Florida

JASON ARONSON INC.
Northvale, New Jersey
London

THE MASTER WORK SERIES

First softcover edition 1995

Copyright © 1972 by Molly Harrower

Library of Congress Cataloging-in-Publication Data

Harrower, Molly, 1906-
    The therapy of poetry / by Molly Harrower.
        p.   cm.
    Originally published : Springfield, Ill. : C C Thomas, 1972
(American lecture series ; publication no. 848. A monograph in
American lectures in psychology)
    Includes bibliographical references.
    ISBN: 1-56821-755-2 (alk. paper)
    1. Poetry--Authorship. 2. Poetry--Therapeutic use.   I. Title.
M1055.H27   1995
808.1—dc20   95-33578

Manufactured in the United States of America. Jason Aronson Inc. offers books and cassettes. For information and catalog write to Jason Aronson Inc., 230 Livingston Street, Northvale, New Jersey 07647.

To those who endorsed and enriched the Poet-Self.

INTRODUCTION

THIS BOOK IS, in a sense, coauthored. The senior partner, a poet; the collaborator, a psychologist. The fact that they both inhabit one physical organism is, I think, incidental, or may actually prove to be helpful to the peculiar task in hand. I, the poet, should not feel threatened by the psychological-self probing into the needs which generate poetic expression. I, the psychologist, will make use of diaries and old letters which reveal usually hidden facets of poem-making. I, the psychologist, will have access to the first drafts and the rough notes enabling me to trace the emerging poem through stages not revealed in the "tidy" versions which see the light of printed day.

Such literary collaboration is, incidentally, not unique. J. M. Barrie, for instance, would frequently speak of McConachie, his "other creative self," an obstreperous individual who sometimes insisted on writing what he wanted, despite Barrie's protests and attempts at control. There is also Hans Zinsser's book *As I Remember Him*, ostensibly a biography of Zinsser's friend, R. S., but as the reader well knows, Zinsser the scientist is writing about Zinsser the poet. R. S. is his Romantic Self.

In such good company we embark on the study of *The Therapy of Poetry*.

CONTENTS

THE
THERAPY
of POETRY

Chapter I

POEMS AND POETS GROW

MUCH HAS BEEN WRITTEN recently about poetry therapy. The assumption being that poetry can be used in numerous ways within the therapeutic hour. Many therapists have attested to this, citing a surprising number of techniques and a wide variety of patient populations (11).

The theme of this book is not so much that poetry can be used in formal therapy, but rather that poetry *is* "therapy" and is part and parcel of normal development. Poetry therapy is a newcomer. Long before there were therapists there were poets, and from time immemorial man has struggled to cope with his inevitable inner turmoil. One way of so coping has been the ballad, the song, the poem. Once crystallized into words, all-engulfing feelings become manageable, and once challenged into explicitness, the burden of the incommunicable becomes less heavy. The very act of creating is a self-sustaining experience, and in the poetic moment the self becomes both the ministering "therapist" and the comforted "patient."

This, in essense, is the burden of my song. This idea has grown with me over the years. It has become more than an idea; it has become a way of living.

One can afford to be hurt, one can afford to reach for the stars, if there is a built-in safeguard against crippling depression or disorganizing excitement.

Another facet of the belief that poetry is part of normal growing is that the rough stages of psychological development, early childhood, the latency period, early teens, adolescence, early and later

3

maturity, seem to be paralleled in the spontaneous output of song, rhyme, verse and poetry written at these times. Early poems, incidentally, reflect a "child is father to the man" motif which, if accepted by the poet as expressing certain idiosyncratic needs, may be used as guide lines for self-understanding.

With this in mind I have begun my study of poet and poem with samples of "song" occurring at the three-year-old level, emerging verse at ages six through ten, the glimmer of a poet's outlook in the early teens, the impact of the adolescent struggle in the midteens and to round out the more strictly developmental stage, I have included poems of the late teens, which seem to be an attempt to reenter childhood, to restate earlier experiences with the perspective of some self-knowledge and greater technical ability. All these phases can be subsumed under the heading of "the *emerging self*."

From there, in young adulthood, there is a phase where the poet-self is conceptualized: "the poet-self discovered." This self has unique responsibilities. Once established, it acquires the freedom to discover the all-important "other." The poet is no longer alone, he is engaged in decreasing the gap between himself and this "other," in "the You-directed poems."

As the variety of life's experiences impinge on the poet, the role of the poem seems to shift to one of sustaining and reinforcing the poet in his task of discovering and maintaining his integrity. Such a phase can be described as the "selfsustaining poems."

Finally, reaching for further growth and groping for new inner worlds to conquer, "the poet-self searches again" in formal therapeutic experiences.

The choice of my own poems, published and unpublished, rather than the works of others as material for this developmental presentation, rests on the fact that to understand poetry's selfsustaining features, or its relation to personal growth, one must know the conditions, specific and general, which trigger the idea of writing a poem, and which allow it to reach a conclusion. For this kind of undertaking one must know the inside story, must be aware of the emotional climate necessary for the emergence of a poem as an entity. One must be able to look at the many unfinished versions which always precede the final product and which are discarded by the editorial self.

In the same way, a longitudinal study is necessary in order that stages of personal and verse-making growth can be recognized.

Although there have been some interesting psychoanalytically oriented postmortems of the works of well-known authors, as for instance that of Lerner on Poe, Whitman and Aiken (12), with the notable exception of Melville Cane (1) very little has been attempted by poets themselves.

This is understandable in that not many poets have an intense interest in their psychological processes per se; moreover, from the point of view of the reader of poetry it is very questionable whether knowing the "inside story" is relevant. It might be said even more strongly that knowing too much about the conditions surrounding the writing of a poem may actually detract from the reader's enjoyment of the poem itself.

One of the prerequisites of true poetry, as opposed to the helpful expression of the "poet's" feelings, is that it transcends the immediate circumstances of its creation, and becomes universal in its application. It is clear that the mature poet has a dual task; he can utilize the built-in mechanism that he possesses for restoring his own inner balance, but also, he must depersonalize this highly charged experience so that others may endow it with their own specific meanings.

How is this dual task developed? How and when does objectivity creep into the process? When is there an indication of the need for poetic form or structure?

Can we, from the inside, throw light on the difference between the "poetic" expression of ideas and feelings (which is essentially a communication between two parts of the self) and a poem which has literary merit? When can a poem be considered as a creation in its own right, one with value apart from the message it gives to the writer or the relief it affords in a tension-filled situation?

It may help to envisage a kind of personal-universal continuum of experience. From the inside it seemed to me that poems which have greater literary value occur at a rather specific point on this continuum. For example, an experience may start as an almost unbearably personal and idiosyncratic segment of living. After a time, however, this same experience may find its place in a much more universal frame of reference. Ultimately it may even lose its personal roots altogether and become virtually an abstraction.

Perhaps the best poems, from a literary point of view, are those which retain a certain amount of highly charged personal feeling, but which become embedded in a more universal approach to life. When a poem is written and *completed* too close to the personal end of the continuum, it may be helpful in handling an overpowering experience, but it will almost certainly have too many specific references, too many immediate details, which have no universality as such, to become a "good" poem.

An extremely personal highly charged love poem in the first stages of writing, for example, will be directed to one person, will almost certainly include references to specific happenings or specific words that have been spoken. It will, at this stage, be a love letter in verse. And while these specificities are pertinent for communication with the beloved, they will be out of place in a larger context, out of place when the reader, the "audience," becomes extended to include all those who have loved or been loved.

For such a wide audience, a poem written and completed too close to the personal end of this continuum will be too intimate, too revealing. Instinctively both writer and reader will feel that its sharing is in poor taste.

On the other hand, when personal experiences have been distilled out altogether, the poem is usually too remote, too guarded, too sterile. The poem will be unrelated to that spark of genuine feeling which must be aroused in the reader or listener as well as in the poet in order that poetry may carry its lyrical message.

Or one might put it in another way, and instead of a personal-universal continuum speak of an intensity gradient of emotional experience. Then as "distance" in time from the emotional earthquake which has sparked the poem increases, the intensity of the need to communicate the experience, *as such,* decreases. From the research psychologist's point of view, it is possible to measure in hours, weeks or months, the times at which poems are written in relation to the initially emotionally charged experience. At the moment of emotional impact, the poignancy and intensity of the situation may be so overwhelming that it prevents clarity of expression, prevents the necessary perspective being taken. Literary merit, then, relates in some way to a hypothetical optimum of emotional intensity and a hypothetical optimum of control.

One can juggle with this concept of emotional intensity on the one hand and control and verbal skill on the other, and hypothesize that there is a point which allows a writer to do his most expert poem-making.

The first version of a poem is often the result of too much pressure. It is imperative to say something at all costs, to reach outward quickly. The controls of form, the economy of wording, the need for clarity, do not operate too well. With the writing of the first version accomplished, pressure is somewhat reduced, and a second version may benefit from a better "ratio" between the need to express and the "how" of this expression.

As the individual matures, as a person and as a craftsman, the early versions of poems are set aside for the time being, they become a necessary stage in the total process, but are rarely the finished product. Poems of adolescence, on the other hand, according to our samples, are rarely revised. The highly charged emotional experience, with all its personal connotations, is considered the end in itself. In many ways poems that are written in the therapeutic setting of "poetry therapy," have this adolescent or too personal quality. Such productions entitle our literary critics to their raised eyebrows, and the question mark which they introduce in "Poetry (?) Therapy." Many poems written within the framework of formal therapeutic experiences have merit as poems, but many do not.

As psychologists interested in therapy and in poetry, we have to be particularly watchful lest we confuse two sets of values. It may be of epoch-making importance to the development of a patient that he be able to express some buried feeling in a form other than prose, but this does not make the product *poetry*.

It is our belief that poems as well as people grow and mature. The stages of this growth have rarely been scrutinized, perhaps because there is a need in all of us to conceive of poems as a gift from the poetic muse. But to understand the therapy of poetry it must be studied realistically, as an integral part of that stage of development that the individual has reached.

Chapter II

THE EMERGING SELF

SMALL CHILD SIMPLICITY

A LEXANDER POPE, the 18th century poet, acknowledges his childhood attempts at verse in the couplet "I lisped in numbers/ For the numbers came." Small children, then as now, do not "write" verses, they say, sing or "lisp" them. It requires an interested parent to catch the sung product. My mother was a faithful and quite busy recorder. What is the small child trying to accomplish in song?

A look at the earliest productions makes one wonder whether, in the making of these songs, we do not have a reflection of one of Erik Erikson's stages of growth, namely, the need to establish *basic trust* as a foundation for further growth. To quote from an edited Symposium in which Erikson spoke:

> For the first component of a healthy personality I nominate a sense of *basic trust,* which I think is an attitude toward oneself and the world derived from the experiences of the first year of life. By "trust" I mean what is commonly implied in reasonable trustfulness as far as others are concerned and a simple sense of trustworthiness as far as oneself is concerned. When I say "basic," I mean that neither this component nor any of those that follow are "worn on the sleeve," either in childhood or in adulthood; they are not, indeed, especially conscious. In fact, all of these criteria, when developed in childhood and when integrated in adulthood, blend into the total personality in such a way that little more than a particular "glow" remains visible. Their crises in childhood, however, and their impairment in adulthood are clearly circumscribed. (2)

Do the songs of the three-year-old reflect, among other attitudes, this basic trust? Here is the first such song, which, according to the diary followed, as a complete non sequitur, to the child asking, "Does Jesus know about my new brown stockings?"

> O the winds do blow
> And the sea is rough
> And the sky is black
> And the winds do crack
> Me, in my bed, I'll safely stay
> Until I see the break of day. Amen.

Despite the black of the sky and the crack of the wind, there is a feeling of security expressed in the line "Me in my bed, I'll safely stay."

Take another song of around that period:

> The daffodils and roses are under the ground
> In the spring they whisper
> "Spring is coming
> And then we'll pop up
>   Spring is coming
> And then we'll pop up
>   Spring is coming
> And then we'll pop up" Amen.

Though momentarily dampened by the winter, the daffodils and the "poet" express their conviction that things will be lively once again. The fact that both these songs end with "Amen" reflects a somewhat watchful, though not necessarily mistrustful, approach. Perhaps it is a whistling in the dark in the face of the immensity of nature!

A year or so later the scope of the subjects chosen to sing about, widens. Visits to unusual places were a stimulus for running comments of this kind:

> Edinburgh with its soldiers bright
> Gleaming on the castle height.

> (Shall I say more?)

Our own, our own, our fortress dear
Guarding us from danger near.

(Shall I say more?)

And by its great Hand
Guarding us and all our land.

Here again it would seem as if trust, or assurance that protection will be given, is one of the motives.

At Seven we have the first transcribed poem, or, as the diary states, "I found a crumpled bit of paper with this on it." This poem seems to reflect Seven-year-old capacity to be part of the growing concern of people of all ages at the threat of war, and is a big step forward in comprehension of what is happening beyond the world of childhood.

Alas the day has come
When war has been declared
In the distance rolls the drum
In the hills the bugles play
Alas, the day has come.

Soldiers have gone forth
To meet the cannon's roar
Some will come back no more
War! War!

Cavalry cantering to and fro
Infantry comes, infantry goes,
Artillery rumbling over the hill
Airoplanes high up over the mill
The little lark now stops to sing:
"War, War is a terrible thing."

THE MASTERY OF RHYME AND RHYTHM

With the first transcribed poem "Alas the day has come" at the Seven-year level, we get a transition to another stage of expressive development. The author attempts more complicated forms, a few changes in wording are inserted. Clearly, a poem that is sung or spoken extemporaneously cannot be corrected, but when lines can be seen, as well as heard, by their author, apparently a rudimentary critical attitude makes its appearance, even at this age.

Another characteristic of this stage is that the poems have names, for instance "My Birthday Party," "My Star." (5)

The achievement of a certain mastery over form and metre at this age level links it with Erikson's feeling that a child needs to master, achieve, work, and by this achievement reinforce his own individuality.

MY BIRTHDAY PARTY

Yes, it will be tomorrow,
  Nurse says at half-past three.
They all will come, their nurses too,
  And they'll have tea with me.

The cake is very, very large,
  With five big candles too.
John has a suit that's sort of green,
  My dress is pinky blue.

Of course, we'll play at hide-and-seek
  Until it's time for tea.
I will show Betty where to hide,
  Because she's only three.

And when it's time for them to go,
  They'll say goodbye to me,
And say they've had a lovely time,
  And such a lovely tea!

This little verse seems to be a good example of the seven/eight-year-old productions. In the original, the actual name of the nurse was present in the second line. There is a concreteness and specificity about these lines which differentiates them from subsequent, and more studied, attempts.

"My Star," written at the same time, is remarkably similar in form and metre. There is structural development here, however, for we get the building up to the concept of a guardian, an all-understanding celestial being. This entity enters into the sadness, happiness of the writer, and exercises some judgmental qualities as well as ultimate understanding. This could be seen as the forerunner of the religious poems which dominate the phase which we have called the Age of Wonder.

MY STAR

I have a very special star,
  He's small and bright
And from up there he watches me
  Through every night.

When I am sad or lonely
  He always knows,
And gives a special wink at me
  To cheer my woes.

When I am very happy
  He is too,
My jokes can make him twinkle
  All night through.

Sometimes when other stars are bright
  Dull is his ray,
That's 'cos I have offended him
  Some time that day.

But he is seldom angry,
  He's really kind,
And if I say I'm sorry.
  He doesn't mind.

Have you a star? (5)

It obviously never entered the ten-year-olds mind that the verse which follows would be published, or bear the adult-oriented title. The fact that it was submitted by the parents to a periodical is evidence of their awareness that, in Erikson's terms, the child needs to experience "achievement that has meaning in the culture." To quote more fully:

In this children cannot be fooled by empty praise and condescending encouragement. They may have to accept artificial bolstering of their self esteem in lieu of something better, but what I call their accruing ego identity gains real strength only from wholehearted and consistent recognition of real accomplishment, that is, achievement that has meaning in their culture. (2, p. 135)

A CHILD'S CALL TO ARMS

In the valley or the street,
Every single lad you meet
Ought to be in khaki clad.
Every single man and lad
Past eighteen, the very age,
Up to forty—quite a sage—
Could join the merry army lads
And get rid of his silly fads.

Don't say "Of course I can't. You see
My business keeps me," or "To me
The army life would be too rough.
You see, I'm not like most men, tough."

You ought to go and say, "I'll come,
I'll lead men, or I'll bang a drum,
I'll ride a horse, I'll march, I'll charge,
I'll fire a gun, I'll row a barge,
I'll make munitions, bridles, caps,
Or big fur coats, like Tundra Lapps."

For England expects you to do your bit,
And I'm sure it will make you very fit,
And young and handsome and strong again,
And save the country from being like Louvain. (3)

Tackling the more difficult subject of recruitment, the ten-year-old seems to have lost some of the more exact and precise formal expression of the "Birthday Party" and "My Star." Along with all other facets of development, it would seem that verse-making also reflects spurts and regressions, and cannot be envisioned as a steady progression to greater maturity.

At this stage we also find seeds of what I have subsequently called the You-directed poems. As in many English households, a figure of enormous importance is the nurse, who, by the very nature of things, must sooner or later give up her charges. When this occurs the little microcosm of the nursery is disrupted and painful parting is the order of the day.

The nurse in this household was openly adored by her charges; poems of praise were written to her at this period! Somewhat to the embarassment of the grown-ups, we children insisted on calling our nurse "Love," and spoke of her, and to her, in this way. Hence, as the horrible moment of parting nears, we find:

> Love is fair and Love is sweet
> Roses I lay at her feet
> She has been mine
> For seven years long
> And never a sign
> Of anything wrong
> O darling Love
> Pray with us stay
> Forever onward
> From this day.

At this time, a small notebook entitled *Poems for Love* provided more outlets for the appreciation of the to-be-departing nurse.

> I'll always love you Lovely sweet
> I'll always make you cakes to eat
> I'll love you always, lovely dear
> And never believe false things I hear.
> I'll love you more than words can tell
> I'll love you when you're ill or well.

And again, when Love married a suitable young man:

> Every word she says is true
> From when she spoke at one or two.
> And always it will be the same
> Right up to when she's made her name
> Her real heroic (!) glorious name

For she has won immortal fame
I knew she would, my darling Love
O dove, O dove, O dove, O dove.

When a substitute nurse was brought in for an interim period, she received a quite different evaluation:

Jessie is smart, and Jessie is neat
Jessie's favorite word is sweet
But to tell you far apart
I could not love her to my heart
As I could Love
I could not brush or comb her hair
I could not take her anywhere
As I could Love.

Verses to "Love" were in a sense a declaration of independence. My brother and I felt in honor bound to champion her. The following exerpt from an autobiographical sketch shows her place in the child-hierarchy of values.

Love had an uncanny knowledge of the infant make-up. On one occasion I was watching my brother, aged one to my four, being bathed. As the slippery little figure was picked out of the tub, to the admiration of my mother and some guests invited to the nursery, I remarked "I wish he were mine." The guests and my mother cooed appreciatively of this sisterly expression of affection. But the clear-eyed "Love" remarked cold bloodedly after they had gone, "I know what you want him for, you want to beat him up." This vindictive thought had, of course, been uppermost in my mind, and while I denied it vehemently the fact that Love KNEW was a tremendously important factor in my feelings towards her, she was clearly omnipotent and worthy of the deepest respect.

One of the few terrible "scenes" that occurred in my childhood centered around Love. As was usual for the families in our small village, we all went to matins on Sunday to the little country church. We had our own pew half way down, and in the center.

At the back of the church were a few pews almost segregated from the main body, and here the maids of the established households had their seats. I have no idea how the custom got started, but, alternately every Sunday, either my brother or I sat with Love in the back seat. It was a firmly established habit, and did much to make Church bearable. If it was not your Sunday to sit behind, then the next one was; somehow the tedious hours were got through on this basis. Of course nothing particular ever happened in the back pews. "Love" was a model of good behavior, and followed the service carefully. It was just that one was with her, all alone, and with the feeling that sitting together like that, one belonged with her.

On the morning of the big black Scene we were getting ready to leave in the front hall. Our pennies had been given to us, and the family and servant contingents were ready to leave, when suddenly, a violent altercation broke out between my brother and me as to whose turn it was to sit with "Love." We always fought each other actively and with much kicking and hitting, and my mother's "Children, children this is Sunday morning" fell on deaf ears. My father, irritated at the idea of Church anyway, demanded to know what the trouble was, and when the argument was explained to him, took the injured view that a fine family he had if his children did not want to sit with him. Always pouring oil on the troubled waters, my mother hastened to add "O no darling, its nothing to do with that, they just enjoy sitting at the back of the church so they can see everyone come in, isn't that so children?" "NO" yelled both children in unison "It's because we love to sit with Love."

Infuriated, my father forbade us ever to sit with Love again. (9)

THE AGE OF WONDER

Poems of the early teens (written between the ages of 11 and 14) reflect a quiescent period within the self which is in sharp contrast to the conflicts and doubts which emerge later.

At this stage we may say that the "self" is hardly involved at all, and that a quiet, controlled mood prevails.

There is an objective approach to subject matter; that which is going on within the self is of little concern. There is an explicit acceptance of the religious and social frame of reference within which the early teen-ager is developing.

Many of the ideas with which the "poet" is concerned are large and rather vague. The poems have such titles as "In The Garden of the World," "To The Spirit of Art," "The Sun," "Dawn," "Change," "To the Hills," "Beauty," "Inspiration," "Faith, Hope and Love," "The Unstained Sword."

In a more prosaic and down to earth mood we find such poems as "The Ballad of Cricket." Nonsense, or light verse, makes its ap-

pearance, as in the exchange between the school girl and the poet
of national repute, A. A. Milne.

IN THE GARDEN OF THE WORLD

I wandered in the Garden of the World,
Where many lives like petal'd buds unfurl'd
And gave their youth and fragrance to the air.

Some burst upon this garden all ablaze
With color and with beauty, bloomed and shot
This fire and color through the tingling air
Till it vibrated, and then died forgot.

While some like roses, clustered, rambled spread
Over the walls of Time, lichened and gray,
And fading lingered still, till petals fell
And only scent and memory could stay.

I turned to leave this garden of the World.
Search as I might I found no doorway there
The old grey walls of time encircled it
I was a prisoner in that garden fair.

In submitting this next poem to the school magazine for publi-
cation the poet was told to take out the word "lover" in the final
lines and substitute "loved one," the former being an "inappro-
priate word for a young girl to use!"

TO THE SPIRIT OF ART

The Artist who created thee must perish!
Too oft his blunted tools of sense
His vision marred:
Sharp-pointed disillusionments
His soul have scarred,
And suffocating fumes of failure lie
Where once burnt flames of vision and desire
Even that vision's essence seems to die
When perishes the mind's creative fire.
But for thee, his spirit child

Born of the everliving mother Beauty
There can be no perishing, no death, no end,
Thou art in essence as the things enduring
Forever will the dawnlight be thy lover
And the great hush of eve will call thee friend.

TO THE HILLS

I lift my eyes unto the hills they stand
A proof for changing earth of God's great might
And, guardians of a luminous beyond
They bar the passage of approaching night.
Enduring strength! Yet it but serves to show
How greater is the tenderness of Love.
They stand unmoved, but see the sunset's glow
Radiant and beautiful, stretches beyond,—above—
So shall God's Love in a like ecstasy
Mount over all filling Eternity.

THE SUN

The Sun's a generous foe!
When he has made a glorious summer's day
Scattered the clouds, and let his radiance play
On all around,
He heralds with a burst of wondrous light
The advent of his swift pursuer Night.

And she is generous too!
For when her loveliness is at its height
The air so still, the stars with beauty bright
She lets her conqueror
His tenderest and his rarest beauty show
And steals away before his saffron glow.

DAWN

Dawn . . . all is still
Gold is the sky over the crested hill
So soft the air, it almost seems a sin
To whisper, ere His Majesty the Sun
Has from his throne declared the day begun.

Noon . . . every thought
Has turned to the common task the day has brought
And men forget the beauties of the dawn,
Life is a rush of troubles joys and care
They have no time to look for beauty there.

Dusk . . . all is still
Shadows and shades fall on the crested hill.
And those whom noon has captured now find rest
And gladdened by the glow of evening light
Pass on content into the silent night.

THE INSPIRATION

Nature in sunset, dawn, and starlit sky
Her beauty shows, that she may draw from man
His own conceptions of the beautiful, which lie
As yet asleep within him. Thus the plan
Of full perfection grows though age and race
Till to a Perfect World, God shows His face.

The artist fired by Nature's power supreme
Captures for men the sunset's dying glow
And in it, gives expression to some dream
Of great perfection, that his mind would show
He leaves for men this beauteous living thought
Lit by the light of Nature which he caught.

The Poet finds in the calm depths of night
That peace and calm for which his spirit yearns
For peace serene with ever cloudless light
Dispels his dark distrust of mind, and turns
His unframed thoughts to beauty's vision clear—
A heritage for all who follow here.

And all men find new life, new love, new zest
New certainty that nothing is too small
For God's great purpose—that to bring our best
Is all He asks us. O, that to the call
Of Nature from resplendent earth and skies
We may respond with all that in us lies.

The religious training which is part and parcel of the British
school system leaves its mark on the poet of these years.

FAITH, HOPE AND LOVE

Faith had gone far
But distant the star
She sought for still remained.
Her strength was worn
She sank forlorn
When in her hour of weakness Hope was born.

Onward they sped
Hope vanquished dread
And yet they failed to reach their goal above
Yet ere their strivings cease
New strength they gain and peace
For on that journey they are joined by Love.

THE UNSTAINED SWORD

An unstained sword is not the soldiers aim.
An unstained soul we cannot hope to bring
After the earthly conflict to our King.

That conflict vain? No. And a broken sword
A braver record of the smallest fight
Than one held back in fear, unbroken, bright.

For God has promised that his fire of Love
Shall purge away all sin, shall cleanse each stain
That in the fight he does command, we gain.

So let us leave in trust this work to Him
Making the soul's increase our one desire
That there may rest pure gold after His fire.

But the mood is by no means always serious or religious. "A
Ballad of Cricket" bears witness to this.

A BALLAD OF CRICKET

Who knows the thrill of Cricket? The Batsman when his score
Has reached a quarter century, and six has followed four.
When runs are coming rapidly, and he has turned the tide
And the luck of his eleven, for his runs will save his side.

So here's to every batsman
Who has steady nerve and pluck
And when his side is losing
Can hit one and turn their luck.

Who knows the thrill of Cricket? The Bowler, when the man
Who seemed set for a century has fallen to his plan.
Or when the scheme he tried for has won his side the match
One run to make, the last man in, stepped out and sent a catch.

So here's to every bowler
Who bowls with head and hand
And who doesn't rate the fielder
Who dropped the catch he planned.

Who knows the thrill of Cricket? The fielder as he waits
With bated breath under the ball that will decide their fates.
And then as in a dream he hears a shout that fate proclaim
He knows the thrill of Cricket; Cricket the greatest game.

So here's to every fielder
Expectant and awake
Who plays the game of Cricket
Just for its own great sake.

Although relatively little has been written on the subject, most poets, we would venture, are almost constantly writing "light verse." Melville Cane devotes a chapter to this in his *Making A Poem* (1), and certainly in the letters and diaries of the "poet" we are scrutinizing, light verse is constantly appearing. What is of interest here is its relatively early appearance, as seen in this fifteen-year-old attempt, written in a letter to A. A. Milne.

Milne's poem was as follows:

James James
Morrison, Morrison
Wheatherby George Dupree
Took great
Care of his mother
Though he was only three.
James James
Said to his mother,
"Mother," he said, said he,
"You must never go down
To the edge of the town
Without consulting me."

It was originally published in the weekly magazine *Punch* and evoked the following from this schoolgirl reader:

M. H. always had
A passion for doggerel verse
But now
Its reached a fever
That's a positive curse.
While looking
Through *Punch*
She discovered a rhyme
And all she will say through all the day is
"This is too sublime."

All her
Letters and essays
Were copied out in rhyme
Her steps went to this metre
She practiced to this time.
If anyone spoke, for answer
All they would get was this:
He's made up a rhyme and the metre's sublime
O rapture, joy and bliss.

They gave
Her "Belinda"
And "Success"
To see
They feared she was going
A little M.A.D.
But no, she responded,
"Excellent books," says she,
"And you're all very kind but I'm quite in my mind
But this is the metre for me."

All day
She sat
Saying it o'er and o'er
"James James
Morrison, Morrison". . .
Friends could stand no more
They vowed
They would
Put her out of sight:
"If you say that again, we will open the drain
And shove you in tonight."

So lost over Morrison's
Troubles she did not hear.
They came and shouted their warning
Loudly in her ear.
She took
No notice
So that her kith and kin

With expressions of pain went and opened that drain
And shoved poor M. H. in!

So ended Molly Harrower
Quite misunderstood
She said
Those verses
All for her neighbor's good.
But they, unrhythmical, snappy and somewhat terse
Nipped in the bud
And drowned in the mud
That passionate lover of verse.

A. A. Milne's reaction was, understandably, "Do I mind having such verses written to me! No, I love it!"

POEMS OF ADOLESCENCE

The soul-searching efforts of the adolescent, the self in turmoil, are a sharp contrast to the peaceful products of the Age of Wonder. While the latter were recorded in a self-made hard-bound volume, the product of a leatherwork class, and were given in pride as a Christmas present, the adolescent poems were entered in diaries marked "Private." Obviously they were considered too revealing of inner pressures and problems to be shown or shared.

In the adolescent poems we see a struggle to achieve a personal identity and to question the very structure of existence which had been so dutifully and prayerfully accepted before.

The "I" now emerges, not as an observer removed from the scene as in "I wandered in the Garden of the World," but as an active participant, with recognized and accepted emotions.

TEMPERAMENT

With heart that ached with the fierce joys of life
I climbed the little hill. There stretched a view
Of fields, which lay in irridescent light
Lit by the spell of mist's ethereal hue.
Brown and bare the hillside—peace, peace sweet
"O leave the world's fierce pleasures at your feet"

Whispered the wind "Find tranquil joys like these
That begin a lasting worth, repose, heart's ease."

I turned—then stood transfixed, before my eye
Stretched an expanse of flaming, throbbing light,
A wind had torn the clouds—an azure sky
Flashed harmony with poppies, poppies bright
Vibrating beauty—Nature's highest art
Lay all around. And O, my fickle heart
In ecstasy forsook its quiet gain
Turning once more to joys akin to pain.

Now we find the poet concerned with problems of changing values, with the experiences of inner conflicts, with the need to safeguard the emerging self.

And men deny a soul!

When all life's stress
Is born within the thought:
I must possess
With all my being what I know is true.
I must embody it and bear the pain,
Though all I hold most dear snaps with the strain.

The texture of my heart
Tears in the strife,
All that my nature holds:
Love ties of life,
And bonds inherent in my being break. . . . .
I feel their jagged pain, I watch them die,
Cut by the soul-steel sword . . . which men deny!

In this phase we also get an indication of how the adolescent realizes he is not alone, and that there are, within his confused and changing universe, other human beings with whom closeness is a possibility. This closeness may not have been achieved, but "true understanding" has been glimpsed, even if not incorporated into daily living.

There is a point in every realm of art
Where truth and beauty meet to kiss love-bound

Where man acknowledges a perfect thing
And reverences this wonder he has found.

There is a moment for each human heart
When vision'd truth beats back on beauty's wings
When all past longing surges and is caught
Enveloped, strengthened, crystallized and taught
The fullness that true understanding brings.

And when these vital human forces meet
Creation's miracles lie at their feet
Known in experience, while the counterpart
Immortalizes man and humanizes art.

The adolescent poems seem to confront the inner turmoil and problems head on. They are excellent examples of what we described as poems written too close to the emotional impact that demands their expression. One knows exactly what crisis the individual is facing. The poems clearly attempt an integration of the new, and often ego-threatening, life experience, with the old and more sanguine beliefs. Take for example the discovery that ideals and idealistic values have an underlying physiological counterpart and are, in fact, part of mechanistic nature:

Men searching for a truth that yields to facts
May show us that our highest thoughts and acts
Are but inevitable cogs and wheels
In that compact machine their search reveals.

If so, fact-sense must bow to their decision.
Even the sunset has its mechanism
Lifeless until our senses give it birth.
All we call "spirit" rises from the earth.

But having risen all its bonds are fractured
What matter than, if thoughts are manufactured
Within this massive moving mystery.
They spell life's very essence, liberty.

The poem restores an inner balance by both acknowledging, and going beyond, the new information that has to be absorbed. It is as if the poet is now entitled to confront life again with optimism. The disquieting truth has been dealt with.

The next poem is a good example, at the adolescent level, of our hypothesis that poems are built-in safeguards. Emotions at this stage can be profoundly disturbing, and the first impact of jealousy has to be coped with.

> Is it that God is jealous? Or how came
> A standard so distorted to exist?
> The world has plenty evils when viewed straight
> We need no warp, we need no fatal list
> Till beauty's self seems disproportionate.
>
> Is Jealousy then god? And beauty slave
> to some capricious passion? Better so
> Than that truth to hypocrisy should yield
> Hiding the values that men seek to know
> By some false colors blazened on its shield.

A typical adolescent crisis is contained in the realization that the grown-ups do not always live up to their own standards or do not, understandably, always practice what they preach!

> From those I honored most I learned in youth
> To build my values round the changless things.
> To hold as sacred loyalty and truth
> To reverence all that love and friendship brings
> To disregard the shallow mundane scale
> And strive for things that live, and cannot fail
>
> How strange! These same I honored most do test
> The potency and worth of their own creed.
> For soon alas, they too raise petty cries
> The mercenary side of life, the ties
> Of social standing, culture . . . . in my pain
> I ask the question Is their creed then vain?

> God kill the thought, I have been given gold
> Of changeless value, give me strength to hold!

Here the struggle for identity is reflected in the need to go against the current, presumably, parental advice. Or, in Erikson's words:

> . . . in adolescence all the sameness and continuities relied on earlier are questioned again . . . . . developing youths are concerned with attempts at consolidating their social roles . . . . . they are preoccupied with what they appear to be in the eyes of others as compared with what they feel they are. Some adolescents have to refight many of the crises of earlier years, and they are ever ready to install lasting idols and ideals as guardians of a final identity. (2)

Religious feelings are expressed in a more sophisticated way than they are in the early teens. At that time there is a conflict-free assertion of a simple faith in a verse such as "The Unstained Sword." Now comes:

> What does it profit man the earth to gain
> And all it holds, if his own soul he lose?
> Nothing: nor does he hesitate to choose
> In place of riches, growth, love, joy, and pain.
>
> But he who saves his soul, whose choice is made
> When the last trump shall sound, how does he feel?
> He who ignores another's mute appeal
> And turns his back on hands that grope for aid.
>
> Who makes the utmost of his earthly lot
> Invests his talents, and as scriptures tell
> In harvesting each corner of his plot
> With garnered sheaves, can prove he did full well.
> If but a part of what he had in store
> He loaned to others . . . . . were the yield not more?

Although obviously not conceptualized in this way, the adolescent is nonetheless pressured to cope with problems of control and impulse. The last poem in this series could be considered the Apollonian-Dionysian controversy in a teenage nutshell:

A long low line of hills . . . . and the sunset's depth
And the Sage said, for Wisdom clogged his soul. . . .
"See how Restraint the essence is of art
These quiet hills will show us mastery
That luminous beyond speaks of a rapture
Comprehended, that the mind may capture
Restraint and beauty come at minds control."

But windswept nature from her depth gave song
"No, see, that cloud holds the epitome
Of all the brightness, which art's simile
Seeks to denote. Man's words are mimicry
They're not the power which gives to life its soul
For here *is* brightness and that pulsing heart
IS more than all the "mastery" of art.

Chapter III

THE EMERGING SELF IN PERSPECTIVE:
CHILDHOOD REVISITED

ENCOURAGED BY A. A. MILNE, our verse-maker became an author, publishing a book with a dedication to Milne's Christopher Robin and written as from the female counterpart, Plain Jane.

> To Christopher Robin
>   Plain Jane must concede
> A pioneer's due:
>   For he took the lead
> In catching those rhymes
> That come constantly bobbin'
> Into one's head,
>   For others to read.
>
> And she hopes that her rhymes
> Which simply just came,
> Won't savour of cribbin'
>   Or otherwise vex,
> It isn't the literary fame
> That she's after
> She feels that she owes it
> Somehow to her sex.

Gone are the highly personal agonies and soul searchings of adolescence. Objectivity has taken over; there is a distance

Note—All verse in this chapter has appeared in *Plain Jane*, New York, Coward McCann, 1929.

achieved between the actual experience and the resulting en-
capsulating of it in verse.

Scanning this volume with the idea of the development of the
individual in mind, several characteristics of the writer seem to
emerge.

One of these is the need for *time to create*, the need for "all
grown-up persons should just go away, and leave me alone, quite
alone for a day, and let me get on with my playing." For, basically,
the creative expression *is* a playful one, for all that it is accom-
panied by certain inevitable routines. The wish, experienced in
childhood, captured by the emerging self, has a lifetime for fur-
ther manifestation.

WISHES

I'm stirrin' the puddin',
And wishin' a wish;
        And what do you think I'm sayin'?
That all grown-up people should just go away
And leave me alone, quite alone, for a day,
        And let me get on with my playin'.

And first I shall play with the Mowin' Machine,
And then I'll make clothes on the Sewin' Machine,
        And I'll jump on my bed,
        And I'll climb on the shed,
There'll be nobody here to say "no" in between.

For my dinner I'll have what I'm wanting to eat,
A big strawberry ice, but no cabbage or meat;
        Then I'll play on the stair,
        There'll be nobody there
To call from the nursery, "Now, Jane, wipe your
        feet."

I'm stirrin' the puddin',
And wishin' a wish;
        And that is the wish I've been sayin',
That all grown-up people should just go away
And leave me alone, quite alone, for a day,
        And let me get on with my playin'.

In these childhood revisited poems there is also the germ of the
conflict between the need to be involved and get busy, to get
things done and to achieve, and the opposing need to get "to the
back of beyond," far from the maddening crowd. "Christmas Pres-
ents" on the one hand, and "Alone" on the other, epitomize these
conflicting pulls. The screen chosen on which to project these
needs and pressures is the nursery world, which the poet remem-
bers vividly.

CHRISTMAS PRESENTS

I'm very very busy
And I haven't time to play
Cos I'm making all my presents
And it's nearly Christmas Day.

I've made a scarf for Daddy,
    It's nearly three feet long;
I've knitted it one plain, one purl,
    It's gone a little wrong.
Do you think he'll mind?

I've made a box for Mummy,
    I've painted it myself
She's got to keep things in it,
    Not put it on a shelf.
I've used six colors,
    But the ink
Has made a smudge
    Across the pink.
Do you think she'll mind?

I've made a little needle book,
    I've also made a purse
And one of them will be for Rose,
    And one of them for Nurse.

But Rose says she's no money
And she hasn't time to sew!
It's really awfully difficult
To get things right, you know.

So I'm very very busy
And I haven't time to play
Cos I'm making all my presents
And it's nearly Christmas Day.

And the opposing need to "get to the back of beyond":

ALONE

We went for a walk alone today,
  Right to the Back of Beyond.
Through the very darkest part of the wood
  Till we came to a teeny wee pond.
And we sat ourselves down on the edge of it
  To talk and think things over.
And I didn't see how there could possibly be
  Anyone else in the world but me and Rover.
Then I started to think of the afternoons
  When Nurse takes us out in the street,
And Rover stops to say "How-do-you-do?"
  To every dog that we meet.
And I see Philip and Margaret and George,
  Who ask me out to tea;
Yes, I suppose there are other folk in the world
  'Sides Rover and me.

A theme that is repeated often is the love of, and identification with animals. The least popular donkey, the stray cat, the over-worked horse. The small child bled for them and their misfortunes, the grown child can now immortalize them for other children.

MUFFIN

Muffin had only one stirrup,
  So nobody wanted him;
He was rather a tired-looking donkey,
  Not frisky like Crumpet or Tim,
  But nobody knew
  What Muffin could do
  'Cept me.

Muffin was only twopence,
  'Cos everyone said he was slow;
And all the others were threepence,
  But I could make Muffin go.
And we used to go galloping over the sand,
Up to the lighthouse, and back to the stand,
  For nobody knew
  What Muffin could do
  'Cept me.

MORE INCONSISTENCIES

I have a box with pennies in
  For all the poor stray dogs and cats;
And everybody says, "Kind Jane,
  It goes to buy them milk and Spratts."

But I got up the other night
  Because a poor stray cat was crying.
It wasn't true he was all right,
  He told me he was nearly dying.
I pushed the window, he jumped in
And cuddled up beneath my chin,
But in the morning—O the din.
  "You might have catched your death of cold,
And them stray cats is full of fleas.
  In future you do what you're told,
And don't you touch the window, please."

So now they've shut it with a catch,
  That's far too high for me to reach;
Will these funny grown-up people
  Ever practise what they preach!

GOING TO THE SEA

I am getting very anxious,
    For we're starting for the sea;
I've a lot to do on journeys,
    And it rather worries me.

They are bumping down the boxes,
And each extra one we bring
    Makes the cab so awful heavy for the horse;
Then the porter won't take care,
Tho' the train is nearly there,
    And Rover's chain gets tangled up, of course.
And I have to say to Nurse
That she mustn't lose her purse,
    Or leave behind the spongecakes for our tea;
And I have my handbag too,
There's an awful lot to do
    When I have to get them safely to the sea.

The poems of this era are full of remembered verbal confusions, remembered incongruous images. However, these ideas have been incorporated into the verses in a different way from the poems which were actually written during the six- to ten-year-old period. A certain technique of depersonalization has been learned. As a young child, for instance, it was the poet's fervent belief that thunder resulted from "God moving his furniture around Heaven." The poem on thunder, however, has kept enough of this idea to become the core of the poem, but it has been handled in a much less personal manner than, for example, "My Star," conceived and written at the earlier age.

THUNDER

When Thunder turns
    In his big armchair
The Moon stops yawning,
    And the stars take care.
When he gets up

And stumps across the sky,
The Wind begins to tremble
    And the Clouds begin to cry.
"I wonder," says Thunder,
    "What Lightning's about."
And the Moon says, "O, sir,
Didn't you know, sir,
    Lightning's just gone out,
Slipped off through that crack,
And she's not coming back,
    However much you shout."
And the Stars add, "Please, sir,
We didn't tease her,
But when you began to wheeze, sir,
    She just ran away."
"I wonder," growls Thunder,
    And sulks all the day.

On the other hand, the small child's concept of the meaning of
work, and the natural confusion of the French "Je t'adore" with
"shut the door" have been kept intact.

WORK

Rose scrubs the Nursery "lino,"
    "And that's work and no mistakes."
Emma scrubs the kitchen steps
    While the dinner bakes.
Maggie has to scrub the stairs
    And the bathroom door.
Daddy works . . . . . I suppose all day,
    He scrubs the Office floor.

SHUT T'DOOR
(Je t'adore)

I had started my bread and honey
    When a Mamselle came to tea.
I had to go down to the drawing-room

> She smiled and said to me:
> "Shut t'door."

> They always fuss about draughts, but
> As a matter of fact the door *was* shut,
> Yet still she kept saying, "Shut t'door."
> Each time I did it they laughed the more;
> That kind of joke is an awful bore,
> It isn't the least bit funny.

In the poems that follow, genuine childhood experiences are recaptured. In the notes which accompany the collection of these verses the late-teen writer states explicitly that in order to have the verses flow, an actual memory had to be evoked. Suggestions which sometimes came from other persons as to their childhood experiences could not be used, or did not "turn into" readily written verses. The rough drafts of these verses, unlike the many versions of later poems, are hardly any different from the finished copies.

PUNCH AND JUDY SHOW

> When I couldn't go
> To the Punch and Judy show,
> The Punch and Judy show
>   Came to me.
> Punch told Daddy that he must see Jane,
> Judy said to Mummy she was sorry for my pain.
> When I couldn't go
> To the Punch and Judy show,
> The Punch and Judy show
>   Came to me.

> If I were Punch I wouldn't be so cross,
>   But if I were Judy I'd be crosser.
> Punch is a disgrace
> "Cos he tried to hit her face,
>   Punch isn't fair
>   "Cos he went and pulled her hair;
> And he'll pinch her, and he'll scratch her.
>   And he'll boss her.

When I couldn't go
To the Punch and Judy show,
The Punch and Judy show
     Came to me.
I told Punch a lot of things quite plain.
And Judy "You just hit him back again."
When I couldn't go
To the Punch and Judy show,
The Punch and Judy show came to me.

---

9 TIMES 7

"9 times 7 is 63,
Look, Miss Watkins, there's a bee
     Climbing up the window-sill,
     Now it's on the daffodil.
9 times 7 is 68 . . ."
"Jane, dear, you must concentrate,
     Turn right round and face the door,
     Start again at 9 times 4."

"9 times 4 is 30 . . . O
There's the mark they made to show
How much more I'm going to grow
     On the door, Miss Watkins, look,
     Daddy put a great big book
On my head" . . . "Attention, Jane,
Face the fire and start again."

I started at 9 times 1,
     I went on till 108,
I didn't stop when the wood went pop,
     And a bit fell out of the grate.
I still kept on when a bit of coal
Jumped out on the mat and burnt a hole.
     You can see how I concentrate!

BATH TIME

"Rose, don't pull up the stopper,
   I don't want to go down the drain.
You never can tell, 'cos I might melt quick,
And you wouldn't have time to get hold of a stick
   To help me get back again.

And think of me swimming up by mistake
   Into somebody else's drain.
And sposin' they just didn't hear me shout,
Or thought they would rather not let me out,
   'Cos, well,' cos they didn't want Jane!"

I'M A WATER BABY

I'm a water baby, a real water baby,
   I can swim ever so far
On my front,
Without anyone holding me up.
Daddy says, "Jane will be winning a cup
   Before we know where we are."

I'm a water baby, a real water baby,
   I believe I was born in the sea.
Mother says,
"Now, little fishy, come out";
But I can't,
I'm a whale, I'm a salmon, a trout,
   And now I'm a mermaid—watch me.

"Gold Talk," so-called at this stage, forms an interesting link with "My Star" and "My Birthday Party" written at the earlier age. This poem was *attempted* at that time but never got beyond the lines about "my mother puts some sparkles in her hair."

GOLD TALK

Sometimes I stay awake at night
　　Till very, very late.
Just once I heard the clock strike ten,
　　Quite often I hear eight.

The house gets quiet, all except
　　The noise I love to hear,
Them talking in the dining-room,
　　Now far away, now near.

They laugh and talk, and sometimes cheer,
　　But that is rather rare;
And on those nights my mother puts
　　Some sparkles in her hair.

The noise they make seems red and gold,
　　I can't hear what they say,
It's just a feeling, and it makes
　　The morning talk seem grey.

Finally, in "Goodnight," a universal experience is well captured.

GOODNIGHT

Mummy, please don't go.
My teeny, weeny toe
　　Is awfully sore.
Mummy, your beads are bright,
Please don't put out the light,
　　Don't shut the door.
Mummy, the blinds aren't drawn,
There's Daddy on the lawn—
Mummy, please don't go,
I specially want to show . . .
　　O Mummy.

Chapter IV

THE POET-SELF DISCOVERED

THE POEMS WRITTEN during the first years of young adulthood seem to represent the making explicit of a discovered self. Gone is the groping and the confusion, the search for solid ground. The tone, the topics, reflect a stage quite different from the struggle for identity. A personal philosophy is being actively developed, a way of life is being charted that is acceptable to this particular individual. The "self" is proving to its own satisfaction that it can stand up to certain pressures, pains, unhappiness, and emerge with flag flying.

> The spiral of my ecstasy and pain
> Has sucked me in its blackest vortex, where
> I see no light, and can but say this prayer:
> "Let me be true to all that I can gain,
> Through this close contact with the living real,
> Gladly each twist and turn of life I'd feel
> Its suffocation and its anguish bear.
> Belief must grow to doubt, and doubt to fresh belief
> A love's fulfillment turn to empty grief
> And back to joy with ever heightened flame:
> The age's swiftness and the moment's length,
> My utter powerlessness and yet my strength
> To see the endless value in this strife . . .
> Yes, I can face the spiral rack of life!"

One might also say that the poet-self is emerging. Certain privileges and responsibilities seem to be assigned to the poet. In a

41

pageant written at this time, including many symbolic and histori-
cal characters, it is the Poet who speaks the opening and closing
lines, and who carries the new message:

The Poet:
>   I ask you to conceive of Time anew!
>   Not some swift tide that ever breaks new ground
>   Leaving behind completed fact as dead.
>   But as a realm, a vast and boundless realm,
>   Its name, "the spirit of a great ideal."
>   Here you will find no future and no past
>   For thoughts and acts eternally exist
>   And shine like stars . . . these stars appear to man
>   When some one mind breaks earthly bonds
>   And joins with this great spirit to create
>   And crystallize some phantom of a dream.
>   Then in his universe man seems a star
>   But these ideals exist before that mind
>   Strove to create them, and indeed shine on
>   When it has ceased in our earth-sense to live.
>   So I would ask you that you view these scenes
>   As stars within the realm of the ideal
>   As living parts of an undying whole.
>   Eternal forces active now as then.

and at the end of the play the Poet again sums up:

>   . . . .
>   You have been audience to these scenes, but all
>   Play in Life's pageant, so to you I call.
>   Remember tis man's mind that must unite
>   With this great spirit ere men see starlight.
>   These words are symbols, aye, and made of dreams
>   But you may pass through moments when it seems
>   That the swift tide of time has no more will
>   Than that of quickening life . . . . that it may kill . . .
>   Then see the universe from this symbolic view
>   Think of this spirit, and conceive of Time anew. (4)

In the poems "Life You Will Lose a Lover When I Die" and "If
I Could Say A Prayer," there seems to be an acceptance of an al-

most privileged position in life to which the poet, by virtue of strong inner feelings, seems to feel entitled.

Life, you will lose a lover when I die!
For whom have you encouraged more; have I
Not always claimed
A thousand burning favors from you,
Proud, untamed and exquisite enchantress?
You say I should not love you, in my face
You have flung hardships, shown me to my place
For my bold daring;
Yet as you spurn me, with the other hand
You cast the colored splendors of the land
For my own keeping; sun and wind and youth
You give me in each kiss. Ah Life, in truth
You will have lost a lover when I die. . . .
But while I live, leave me this ecstasy. (7)

If I could say a prayer
(I who have found so much of beauty
In things actual,
That I have ceased to yearn for what might be),
Then standing with head bare,
"God," I would cry to Thee,
"Take thou my happiness
Too great for me to hold.
Now in its blazing splendor
Lest when I'm dying, old,
I've lost life's vibrant ecstasy."
And I would give this gift
When youth's fierce sun is high,
While I can cry:
"I laugh, I live, I love,
I cannot die."
And for myself I'll keep
Its counterpart of pain,
A measure of intensity to be

A standard for my life's integrity,
Thus I create and claim my immortality. (7)

The dominant mood is buoyant; life and living are celebrated.
Actual existence, the here and now, are honored.

Little you comfort me forsooth
Time-honored abstract of my strivings . . . Truth!
How can my little bricks of fact
Create and fashion thee
Whose structure is eternal time
A whole I cannot see . . .
And yet with all my optimistic youth
I'll fight for something
And I'll damn you Truth
If you elude me so . . .
For I am one with life,
Its flux and flow
Blends with my body
And my mind may grow
Create and fashion thoughts alive and new.
Thus am I one with life,
And more than she,
For in her pulsing eager pace
She knows not her bright form and face
Knows not the joy they give . . .
She moves unchecked, but for a space
Of years, I step aside and trace
My movements in this headlong race
I 'understand' and 'live.' (6)

Finally, we get what might be called an invocation: live this
way because it is suitable, for you, as a poet, so to do.

TO THE POET

Be not afraid.
Let Beauty walk with you,
Leading you where she will.
Go undismayed.
If she would talk with you,

Listen and learn, until
Her haunting song you can no longer bear.
These insights that she calls on you to share
Must be relayed,
Translated to all men, and yours this task,
The reason for her trust you must not ask.
Nor need you question why you are thus blessed.
And, as the sword of time hangs o'er your head,
You will with very desperate haste be pressed.
Breathless, exhausted, you will know not rest,
But vision and bright joy you'll have instead.
There will be time for peace when you are dead. (7)

Chapter V

THE POET-SELF FINDS WINGS

ONCE THE POET'S IDENTITY has been established, once the personal philosophy and orientation to life have been achieved, there seems to be boundless energy to pour into the delights of living and to the initial discovery of the "other person." The early adult poems are hymns of praise, they are outpourings of gratitude for a state of being that seems unthreatened and eternal.

Erikson makes a similar observation on the first stage of adulthood:

> . . . but it is only after a reasonable sense of identity has been established that the real intimacy with the other sex is possible. Sexual intimacy is only part of what I have in mind, for it is obvious that sexual intimacies do not always wait for the ability to develop a true and mutual psychological intimacy with another person. What I have in mind is that need for a kind of fusion with the essence of other people. (2)

In this first stage of adulthood no shadow of conflict appears. The You, You, You brings endless joy. There is no need for the poet even to think of loss, temporary or permanent. The poet is unaware of potential tragedy, the sky is cloudless. For example:

> This skein of love
> I hold within my hands
> Is woven fine,
> With many colored strands
> That run the gamut

46

Of the rainbow's hues,
The burning reds,
Unfathomable blues,
The yellows of clear joy,
The ever-green
With threads of lustrous gold
And silver sheen.
And I can draw at will,
Embroidering the design
That best will integrate
Your life and mine.
What will not blend with both
I need not use,
Such the variety
From which to choose.

Or again,

Bright star in the sky,
Bright joy in my heart!
More enduring than I
Are you, star in the sky,
For the light you impart
Has been there since the start
Of the cosmos, and must
Be there when I die
And am rendered to dust.

But this joy in my heart,
O star in dark night,
Though doomed to depart
In oblivion's abyss,
To me is as bright
As your eon-old light,
For star, tell me this:
Did the being you love
Light your lamp with a kiss?

You have worked miracles with Time!
For when our lives have blended
That piercing ecstasy has split the minute
And shown me the eternity within it
So that the future and the past are ended
And I possessor of all Time can give.

You have worked miracles with Space
For since my thoughts have entered
The open highways of the searching mind
Our tracks are common, and tis you I find
At every turning, and my life is centered
And I possessor of all you can give.

And what are these but words
And can a phrase
Do ought but terminate
The self expression maze
That has ensnared me. . . . .
This is not my aim
What I would do
Is shout from the hill tops,
Laugh the whole world through
That I am happy, with, by and in you.

And, in a similar vein:

I keep no record of my days with you.
'Twere sacrilege to chronicle such happiness,
What if I changed?
Might not some future hard-eyed self review,
Attempt to understand, and reconstruct anew
Durable fabric from this golden dew.

I need no record of my days with you!
Though time erases clear-cut memory!
For while I live
My being gains a rich summative tone
Inherent in my very flesh and bone,
Born of this happiness, and thus my own.
I want no record of my days with you! (6)

But the sky cannot remain cloudless. Sooner or later the threat of loss, the threat of something less than eternal bliss, makes itself known. As a result of emerging from a transient period of stress a mood prevails which triggers a special type of poem. *Recaptured* happiness is the dominant note, and the poems reflect a bittersweet, a reprieve from deepest sorrow, a rebirth of ecstasy.

> O very gracious friend, companion dear and lover,
> You who walk with me through the woods of life,
> I have lost you somewhere in this tangled thicket.
> I have stood naked in the rising storm of anguish
> And have cried out for you; yet when you came,
> Thoughtless I let the stems snap back into your face
> And caused you pain.
> O very gracious friend, companion dear and lover,
> Break with the morning of your love across this night
> And lose me not again. (6)

> I have slipped my hand into yours
> And the night is past,
> Night of doubting and darkness,
> Misgiving and pain.
> Your fingers have closed on mine
> And the sun at last
> Has risen again.
>
> I have slipped my hand into yours
> With my fingers curled,
> Warm and relaxed in your palm
> As young birds safe in their nest.
> Halt your swift passage, O Time,
> Cease to revolve now, World,
> I am so richly blessed. (7)

Swift my awakened thoughts as swallow's flight;
And the earth's freshness after summer rain
Holds something of the joy I feel again
When my mind breaks from the imprisoning night.
And as the sun and wind will kiss the grain,
And wanton waves of shimmering gladness flow
Across this field and that, thus do I know
Freedom and motion after numbing pain.
O that the hearts of those now tied by fears
And weariness and anguish past belief,
The homeless and embittered, whom the years
Have throttled in the stranglehold of grief,
May somehow for this reawakening yearn,
Holding the hope that beauty may return. (7)

Darling, you must know
The day you go
Stretches, a waste of snow,
Or sand when the tide is low.
While mind is dormant and the pulse is slow.
Thus nature in retreat
Immobile, numb
Awaits returning heat
Awaits tide's inward flow
Awaits time's tribal drum
To pound expectant beat
The day you come.

The flood gates of my heart are open
And for miles around the land is green
The life-giving, long imprisoned, waters
Now move outward to fulfill their destiny.
And the land and the water
And my heart, and that which it will accomplish,
Sing in harmony

For now I know that love cannot die
Out of pain and faith has sprung fulfillment.

Long have I shunned
Despised
The second best
The compromised
In love and living.
Rather come fast and prayer
Than not to share
Splendors of giving.

Thus has your presence brought
More than the rapture sought
In lovers mated.
A meaning re-inforced
A way of life endorsed
A truth re-stated.

APRIL

First spring I know!
God made it so,
The flowers grow
And there is warmth and light and laughter.
What could be otherwise?
What else the framework
Of love's world comprise?
Who could envisage frost and death thereafter?

Who could foretell from April's loveliness
The lonely terror of the ice-bound earth?
Or who believe from winter's barrenness
Could come the marvel of the spring's rebirth?

Or that the long dead heart
Could reawake and sing?
Here is the very miracle,
Love's second spring. (7)

The recurrent theme of this period, found, lost, found again is expressed in "Second Bloom":

Now at your touch
The roses bloom again!
They gathered much
From sunshine and from rain
The summer long.
June saw them climaxed
And then saw them die.

Now with the magic
Of your fingers strong
To prune, to bind
To cherish and to tie
The tender shoots . . .
The dowdy brushes
Burst to rich red song
These last days of July.

Chapter VI

NOTES ON THE "WHY" OF WRITING

THE "WHY" OF WRITING engages the poet-self at this time, as letters indicate:

I write poems because they solve a conflict, because I am ill at ease spiritually and want to clarify my thoughts and feelings. I write poems because from some inner chaos, I am driven to create order. I write poems because I am flooded, overpowered by feelings which have been provoked by some aspect of life or nature. This great bulk of feeling can only be subdued or brought under control if I allow some intellectual craftsmanship to work on it, to produce a manageable thought which I can control in the place of the all-pervading emotions which control me.

I can give you a recent example of such a conflict—a conflict which at first sight has no solution, and therefore causes this unrest; a conflict which is finally intellectualized, analyzed and to some extent, at least for one person, is solved in the poem:

CHRISTMAS 1941

Across the earth a giant specter stalks
Specter of famine: not of bread alone
But of the truth;
Across the sun a dread eclipse has passed
And death lies in the shadow it has cast
Death of man's spirit and integrity.

Note—This chapter is from letters written by the author.

And locked in conflict those who would be free
And those who would impose this rule of night
Negation, hatred, force and pagan might.

We cannot sing in praise, because our land
Is rich, its sun still bright.
Their fight is ours, and thus vicariously
We suffer blow for blow with those who stand
And offer broken thwarted lives for liberty.

But we may praise, and fierce may be our joy
That in past years, which naught can now destroy
We were vouchsafed the chance to work, to strive,
The chance to throw our weight against a yoke
The chance to give ourselves to a campaign
That brings no conquest, save of suffering
No subjugation save disease and pain.
And in these vital years of strength and youth
Could burn our candles at the shrine of truth.

In this poem the only thing which could really solve the conflict
would be some legitimate reason for joy and thanksgiving at this
joyous season, namely, an end to war. Just what our individual
part is or should be in this great struggle must be in our minds all
the time; but it is brought to a head and rendered acute by the
knowledge of the sufferings of millions at this Christmas season.

I admit, as I said, that the solution is my personal one, for being
able to pursue research is the privilege of one particular individ-
ual. But the poem is perhaps, or at least I hope it might be, more
than that for it is a thanks offering for all persons who, in these
recent war years, in some form or another, have been permitted
by circumstances to be constructive rather than inactive, able to
function rather than held in suspension.

Conflicts obviously take different forms at different stages of
one's development, but it seems that the common denominator at
any stage is the fact that, by their expression, by the very fact that
they "emerged," some positive approach to life is achieved in the
face of an apparent dilemma.

Take "Spiral" (see page 41) which I wrote some years ago; here the paradoxes of life's happiness and unhappiness, its great moments and its moments of despair, if simply experienced side by side, would be frightening in their meaninglessness. "What is the point of all this?" the passive experiencing individual might cry out again and again. But "Spiral" attempts a framework, indicates a pattern of existence, offers one solution to the riddle. For if in the spiral of growth both these aspects of life are necessary in order that we move or develop, then life is not meaningless but essentially meaningful, and what must be borne must be borne gladly as an intrinsic part of the whole.

Or take the poem evoked by the frightening experience of being seriously ill in hospital several years ago:

> Only my conscious clock that ticks
> To the relentless throbbing of my pain.
> Yet must this pulse I cherish beat in vain
> Smothered in something sinister and still
> For death, with iron stride, can nightly pace
> The ward at will.
>
> "Death" they have said with such complacency,
> "To the Eternal Haven, pass we must!"
> Passive they would surrender life . . . that death
> May add it to his pile of nothingness and dust!
>
> Tick on then, conscious clock
> To the relentless throbbing of my pain.
> Gather momentum with each beat,
> That when I'm face to face with Death, the cheat,
> Though I be crippled, speechless, yet I still may fight,
> Making a dagger of my burning hate,
> Wielding it with my will,
> And thus, at bay, at least to wound the hand
> That makes me nothing, sinister and still.

Perhaps you would not call this conflict in the usual sense, but there seems to be an attempt to wring something positive, at least temporarily, out of the ultimately and inevitably defeating experience.

But it is not always necessary to make the conflict explicit in the poem. Sometimes one word will be sufficient to set the stage, for by its meaning alone it will sound the challenge. You know my poem:

> This loneliness shall be a sacred thing
> As pregnant with your spirit
> As the hours when you are here.
> Thus do the dark days merit
> All the swift gladness that your touch can bring
> And I, through life, inherit
> The naked flame of joy, your presence dear.

The opening line "This loneliness shall be a sacred thing," demands that the thought be developed so that there is triumph in the climax.

And I think you can see the same thing in the poem, "I keep no record of my days with you" (page 48). Here is an attempt to get even with the fleeting days of happiness which are sucked away into the past and of which no record can be kept.

In short, much of my poetry springs from the inner need to set thoughts and feelings in order and to emerge triumphant from difficulties. And if I look back at my old poems, poems written in adolescence, I can see the same processes at work. I remember getting the worst shocks having to adjust to more new ideas, seeing things I believed in crumble, more often then than at any time since. I remember how desperately I tried to emerge with something to live by, how I tried to escape from drowning in the deluge of new and conflicting ideas. For example:

> Little enough we hold
> For change, life's essence must
> Wither and turn to dust
> The things of gold.
> But we may bind unto our very being
> That rare capacity for beauty-seeing
> And thoughts which make the heart
> Leap with their very potency.
> Sayings of men who caught

A drop of life within a crystal bowl.
Sayings we keep, as fibers for the soul.

All these mixed metaphors make me shudder now, but I see what I was trying to say, and was struggling for.

Also in those days there was the paradox of realizing that one's verbal ability, one's rhyme-making capacity which had up to then stood one in good stead, got one good marks and prizes as a child, might now be defeating its own purpose. Something beyond verse-making was needed. The poem I called "The Balance" epitomized this thought and to some extent solved the dilemma.

My world is at its spring
My mind in fancy plays
Carving a skillful thing
A clear-cut chiselled phrase
From the wrought stone of Life.
And men will praise
Me undeservedly, 'tis they would give
Real meaning to my words,
They make them live.

Then will the balance swing!
When *I* have lived, and fain
Would shape and intellectualize my hurt.
Although my vast and formless mass of pain
Is living matter, yet my mind inert
Creates no living thing; nor can it show
The things that heart and mind and spirit know. (6)

Reading this over it looks as if so much of life hurt! But when I speak of being flooded, or overpowered by feeling, such feeling is as often as not an ecstatic one. Then the poem becomes a sort of protection from the violence of the emotion. Or the poem becomes a thank offering for the privilege of having the emotion. Something says "if you have had this happiness, it is your duty to crystallize it, to externalize it so that others can share it." "Life You Will Lose a Lover When I Die" (page 43) is a good example of this ecstasy, as is also "If I Could Say a Prayer" and my first reaction to New England:

Earth hold me in the hollow of your hand
Let me express
Your great austerity
Your tenderness.
Carefree your loveliness
As that of youth
"I am the absolute" you cry
"And I defy
The searchers for a systematic truth."

Perfect with form and line
Where myriad twigs entwine
As in fine filigree they trace
Some craftsman's fancy on the golden space.

Color that holds my heart
Prisoner in ecstasy
Birches that slash me with their living white
Touching my pent-up pain.
Skies that unite
With smothered thoughts
And bring them back to light
Tearing aside the tight
Dark sheathes of numbness
That have dimmed my sight.

Earth hold me in the hollow of your hand
Enough for me
That I have felt and have expressed
my love for you,
And all the pain and rest
You give. (6)

When I say poems are provoked by some aspect of life or nature
I also mean a *person* who can evoke the feeling that "demands" a
poem. Perhaps a person more than anything else evokes the over-
powering pressure. I suppose that is why people say that a poet
seems perpetually in love, because when one is in love one is un-
usually sensitive to facets of another's character. One sees a per-
son as standing for abstract and intangible values which are

greater or more universal than the person himself . . . values
which are crystallized in demonstrable behavior. For instance:

> You waste no words, you make no map of life
> You lie not sleepless at the "why" of things
> For you the very struggle of the climb
> Out-values vistas that the summit brings
> Of peak on peak, and the sun's flashing sword.
> You seek no crowning splendor, no reward
> No final triumph of some greater power.
> But bare intrinsic beauty hour by hour
> Create in all you do, because you must.
> And almost more than love for you, and trust,
> I needs must honor this integrity. (6)

Or,

> I talk too fast, they cannot speak to me
> The myriad little things:
> I walk with purpose to a goal I see
> And I must bruise the wings
> Of all the little things
> In passing.
>
> The leaf, that spirals wanton in the wind
> The hush that follows on a banging door
> A single phrase within a well-loved book
> A lamp-flung shadow on a polished floor.
> These myriad little things speak not with me
> But wait for your long fingers to caress them
> You who seek not to marshall them in ranks
> But only watch them tenderly, and bless them. (6)

Or the poem on the death of the brilliant student I told you
about, who was killed a few days after graduating:

> O young Saint George
> In shining mail
> Standing upon the threshold of your life.
> Your bright steel blade uplifted in your fight

On dragons of warped thought, the cheap, the trite.
Gone, ere you could have conquered in one fight.

O young Saint George
You will not know
Frustration, failure, or the loss of faith.
The gall of being called upon to yield.
You will find worlds to conquer as you prayed
And in the mighty army of the dead
The sun will still pick out your golden head
Integrity is blazoned on your shield
And you will find your place, undaunted, unafraid. (7)

Three different people, but they all demanded a poem!

Chapter VII

THE YOU-DIRECTED POEMS

IN THE You-directed poems there is a slight shift of emphasis. The major source of stimulation, or the source of the pressure to verbalize, is the jubilant immortalizing of the beloved. Poems at this stage crescendo to the "You."

As pigeon circles, wider, wider yet
Hither and yon, lost and directionless,
Baffled, frustrated, till this very stress
Creates his compass and his course is set.
As the exhausted fox or hunted hare
Sidetracks the hounds, crossing at river's race
Losing the anguished panic of the chase
In the accustomed shelter of his lair,
So do my thoughts, straining in emptiness
Beat frenzied wings, lost birds in alien sky;
Or chased by phantom hounds of loneliness
Vicariously, a thousand deaths they die,
Till, freed of fear by homing instinct true,
Swift and unerring they return to you.

And my soul like a prison'd bird
Flies through the vast halls of my loneliness,

Note—Most of the poems in this chapter are drawn from *Time to Squander, Time to Reap*, New Bedford, Reynolds DeWalt Printing, 1946 and 1965.

And 'gainst the windows beats its bruised wings
Kept from the air and freedom that is you.

I must have time to tender to each day
Specific recognition of its bliss,
Be it held in the spotlight of your kiss
Or be it only setting for the play.
I must have time to greet, as friend, well known,
Each rounded hour; the wayward minutes catch
As they dance by, I must have time to match
Their antics in a wild dance of my own.
I must have time to squander, time to reap
Belated harvest periled by the frost,
Time to recapture visions I have lost.
I must have time for nothingness, for sleep
In order that each day I wake anew
To its full burst of glory . . . . and to you.

The pressure lies in the need to communicate the turbulent
feelings. We shall see later that there are poems arising from "neg-
ative" pressures, from despair and anguish, the writing of which
is an attempt to ward off paralyzing depression. But in this in-
stance the balancing act achieved by the writing of the poem re-
lates to the control of overexuberance and the heightening of the
capacity to establish closeness with another person.

You who have shown me what it means to live
With sunset splendor, who have let me share
Your gallantry of being, and laid bare
Transcendent beauty in the love you give.

You who have meant for me intensest prayer,
You who embody triumph over all;
Just as the scarlet maple greets the fall
Do you fling colored courage everywhere.

But I, who gain from you a boundless power,
Must frame the infinite within a phrase,

Rigid and lifeless, and in finite ways
Make timeless love explicit in an hour.

This need to communicate is an integral part of the experience of creating the poem. It is a need to share, not an exhibitionistic need. It does not have the feeling "look at what I have written, it's a good poem," at all. Rather the poem needs to be shown, even if it is not good. It is more a feeling of an unspoken footnote to the beloved: "Look, you mean this much to me so that this utterly unpredictable, uncommandable pressure has suddenly been turned on." It may also mean something like this: "Don't be afraid that you have liberated something I can't handle."

To watch the lights and shadows on your face,
To see stern lines of quiet mastery
Break in your smile of warmth and tenderness.
To thrust the steel of my endeavor's blade
Into the white flame of your honesty,
To temper and to test my own integrity.

To view the gothic arches of your mind,
Devoid of all baroque verbosity,
And in their grace and strength and clarity
To find the architecture and the plan
That gives a meaning to the hours I spend
In my attempt to build a home for truth.

Sometimes a wild delight is on your face,
And as you toss dark curls upon your brow
You look like some bronzed woodland satyr. Now
You move with a leashed power, precision, grace
As leopard lunges, as a panther springs
Upon its prey, or rallies to its mate.
Then of an instant smould'ring fires abate,
And your pure profile, as Egyptian king's
In death, is noble and serene. I trace
Economy of line, beauty as straight

As Euclid of passions, yet compassionate,
Devoid of self, yet holding in self's place
The joys and woes of all the human race.

The pressure to capture and immortalize the You combines with excitement triggered by natural beauties; unexpected and spectacular sights or sounds become a background in which to embed, or offset, the qualities of the beloved.

See how the sun
With a great gesture
Tears the clouds apart
Laughs on the solemn hill
And turns the saddened grain to burnished gold.
So thoughts of you
Will sweep in splendor
O'er my mind and heart
A flood of light to fill
My spirit with your presence as of old!

and again,

I see you as the soaring lark must see
The rolling hills lit from the sun-drenched west.
Dark clumps of trees, the patch-work fields of grain,
The quiet river stretched across the plain,
A heavy silver necklace on earth's breast.

I see you as the soaring lark must see. . . .
(Tremulous lark in scintillating blue)
The very framework of the world. The farm
That nestles close under the hill's crooked arm
With barn and hayrick to her bosom pressed.

Even at lonely heights the lark can see
The rich maturing wisdom of earth's face,
And, tiny dot in space, with whirring wing
For very rapture will explode, and sing
Her meaning; growth and plenty, joy and rest.

Your love is as the good earth
Providing rich and abundant nourishment
To that which seeks to grow.

Your love is as the cherishing sun
Of southern climes
So that the blossoms of thought and feeling
Confident of clemency
Grown lavishly, daringly
Touching the extremes of their potential beauty.

Your love is as the breeze that stirs
Dispersing the blight of inaction
Adding another dimension
In the patterned movements of the branches
As they respond to your touch.

You make of your love an atmosphere
In it, that which lives and grows hesitantly
May attain its full perfection
And achieve its destiny.

Sometimes it would appear as if the writing of a You-directed poem springs from the need to give a more permanent place in the universal scheme of things to one particular love-experience. The widest possible setting is evoked to contain, and to safeguard the ephemeral moment, to give proper dignity to the time-vulnerable experience. Lines such as "thus spun through eternity's fabric my loving you," and "for only in eternity can live the penetrating beauty that you give, which is both life and that life's answered prayer," are good examples.

The burden of my love for you must grow
With each fresh insight, each new spirit gain,
And numbed with gladness, only tears can show
How strong its pressure, exquisite its pain.
The more I live, more fully do I know
The meaning of your poignant tenderness,
Awed by its beauty, trembling I can trace
A boundless, timeless love within your face,

Such that I scorn to crave stability,
I need it not, I hold eternity. (6)

If I could love you now for the first time!
And to those joy-bewildered moments bring
The strange serenity of sorrowing.

If I could love you now for the first time!
Then could chaotic thought that fineness gain
That comes from loneliness and parting's pain.

If I could love you now . . . but who can tell,
Perhaps suspended between Heaven and Hell,
Caught between my despair and clear belief,
Caught between gladness and this cramp of grief . . .
I could not speak . . . my spirit would be dumb.

O God, if God there be!
Though I can live both phases, yet to Thee
I leave the keeping of their greater sum. (6)

I have woven the web of my love
On the loom of years.
Its texture: intangible beauty,
Joy wedded with tears.
Its pattern: the growth of my spirit.
Like sunset, its hue.
Thus spun through eternity's fabric . . .
My loving for you. (6)

I want to take your face within my hands,
To push my fingers slowly through your hair,

To rest my lips on yours, till the suspense
Of sharp ecstasy I cannot bear.
I want to cry and in that cry to tear
My loving free from space and time's pretense;
For only in eternity can live
This penetrating beauty that you give,
Which is both life, and that life's answered prayer. (6)

Certainly it can be said
In the garden of the little French restaurant
Under the plane trees
When lips and wine are red.
But remember, it will take on the color
Of the evening and its surroundings
It will be infused with gaiety
It will include the pressure of hands
The touch of knees under the bright cloth,
What you have said will be the peg
On which all these delightful sensations can be hung.

Certainly it can be said
In the peace that follows passion
As a final proclamation
To the sharp trumpet call of ecstatic joy.
But remember, it will be but one line of melody
In the great symphony
It may be lost in the crashing chords
In the roll of drums
In the compelling surge of power of the strings,
In the lilt of the flute and oboe
Of the body, become orchestra.

How then should it be said,
It should be whispered
In the grey dawn,
Before the sun has restored to us color
Of the birds reminded us of music.
It should be said when the beloved sleeps

> As benediction
> And as prayer of gratitude
> For in these words the speaker
> Proclaims his hold on life eternal.

A clearly demarked stage in the You-directed poems are the poems which reflect a pressure to establish a You-Me achievement, a *joint experience* which is a joint creation. It is not enough, during these moments, for the poet to immortalize the You. Rather, what must be captured are those facets of experience which have resulted in a mutual achievement.

Whereas in the first phase of the You-directed poems the poet stood off, was awed and worshipped, the pressure now is to preserve those aspects of the experience in which the poet was a true partner. Immortality, the capturing of the moment in words and phrases, must have the quality of the "We," not the "You."

Erikson's second stage of adulthood closely parallels this. Just as we found the *need for intimacy*, his first stage of adulthood, to be the counterpart of our "The Poet-Self Finds Wings," so his concept of *Generativity* seems to have a poetic counterpart also. Erikson writes:

> Generativity is primarily the interest in establishing and guiding the next generation, although there are people who, from misfortune or *because of special and genuine gifts in other directions, do not apply this drive to offspring but to other formal creativity, which may absorb their kind of parental responsibility*. The principal thing is to realize that this is a stage of the growth of the healthy personality and that where such enrichment fails altogether, regression from generativity to an obsessive need for pseudo intimacy takes place, often with a prevading sense of stagnation and interpersonal impoverishment. (2, p. 142–143)

A typical poem illustrating the need for sharing:

> I want to share with you the things I see!
> No more can young leaf-green, audacious red
> Cloud-blue of hill and desert turn my head,
> Something is lacking in my ecstasy.
> I want to share with you the things I feel!

No longer can the sun or wind's caress
Lull me with magic fantasies, the real
Lies in your finger tips, to stir and bless,
I want to share with you the things I own!
The age-old insights, gifts to womankind,
My individual blend of heart and mind,
The residue of glories I have known.
I want to be the soil for seeds you sow,
I want your soil that my deep roots may grow.

Let me but once
And for all time, speak
The words unsaid at your departure.
Words held back,
    Lest against the din of traffic
On an exposed street corner,
Or beside the hasty breakfast cup
And scattered morning paper,
They may appear theatrical
And their solemnity incongruous.

Dearest of Beings
    You who give meaning warmth and depth
To all I do
Live in my heart today
And let me live in yours.
Forgive the demands of a too-hungry love
Fraught with the dangers of possessiveness
But grant me the right to safeguard
From all the inroads of destructive doubt
And all the accidents of happenstance
That inner closeness
And that freedom of the spirit
Which is yours and mine, which is *you and me.*

You have sown seeds of many truths in me:
And some have flowered at once in consciousness
So that I cry, "This, this you have giv'n."
But others may lie dormant through the years,
Till of a sudden, grown within the soil
Of loneliness, opens this bud of yours.

You give me insight to a strange serenity,
A consciousness beyond experienced thought,
Beyond the flux of intellectual strife.
A certainty more real, more ultimate
Even than feeling's tempest violence. . . .
This power within me that can never die.

———————————————

As flowers in shade must turn towards the sun,
So I am drawn to you
For all the light and warmth that makes for growth.

As roots are thrust into the fertile soil,
So would I reach for you
For all the nourishment my spirit craves.

As tendrils touch and curve and climb,
So would I hold to you;
Not with possession's fierce and strangling grip,
But resting lightly on your outstretched boughs
Grow to the stature that has been ordained,
Achieve the promise that within me lies,
And bring forth fruits of full maturity.

———————————————

With all your inward and intrinsic grace,
With hands as exquisite and dear
As the love mysterious they trace,
And with a light pellucid in your face
From sorrows and from joys to me unknown,

You welcomed me.
And fearless, I, with breathless joy, laid bare
My loyalty, my love, my youth,
And held it as an answered prayer
That vision'd beauty was made actual there,
And with a quality perhaps my own
I came to you.

I have looked deep in many pairs of eyes.
Some show bewilderment and their distress;
Some draw quick curtains lest perchance I guess
The goals they cherish, or the gems they prize,   .
In some a wave of tenderness will rise;
In others there is peace, after fierce storms;
In some the miracle that love performs
When the soul's wealth and richness in them lies.
But you have answered smile with candid smile,
Have flung my laughing challenge back at me
No secrets, no enigmas to beguile,
But pungent humor, salty as the sea,
And with the tang of spray. In our eyes meeting
It is as if twin suns had flashed a greeting.

Finally the You-directed poems, the poems of praise, the mutual
achieving, the immortalizing of a specific experience, give place
to a concept of love that is broadened and deepened. There is a
shift towards a more universal experience. The immediacy of the
bond with the beloved has become less vital, less necessary. What
the poet seeks has changed.

> To look on things with love,
> And in that loving share
> Pathos and beauty rare
> That has been harbored there.

> To look on things with love,
> And in that loving hold

All time, the new, the old,
The heavens which unfold.

To look on things with love,
And with that loving bring
Triumphant peals that ring
Death to death's challenging.

Love is no longer
desire for possession,
or even the need for companionship.
It is that which is released, called into being, within me.

I love you because your image of me
comes close to what I want to be,
can be, know that in some way, I am.
Because your estimate is both
realistic and idealistic,
Because I am dear to you
not only for what I am
but for what I may become—
Because you sense
the struggles and the triumph
of the invisible and indelible past
Because you make concrete for me
the next step in my self-conscious development.

Love is no longer
desire for possession
of you, or of anyone.
It is light to live by
It is, in one shattering moment, meaning, understanding.

Chapter VIII

NOTES ON THE "HOW" OF WRITING

DIARIES AND LETTERS at this stage seem to be more concerned with the "how" of writing:

For days before I begin to write I am aware that something is brewing. I am distressed, but don't know why. Sometimes I feel actually physically ill, and then, all of a sudden, one single phrase will pop into my head from nowhere . . . a line, or a few words, and I will recognize it as the epitome of the vague struggle that I have been experiencing. The unconscious yields up a fragment of what has been churning inside and says "Now, that's yours, go on from there."

Then a totally different task begins. In the place of the vague unrest comes an overpowering desire to set down words. I must have pencils and paper, masses of it. Time and time again I put down just that line which has suddenly come to mind, just that, nothing else, and finally I see it as part of a poem of a certain length and kind. Perhaps it is the very last line and must be preceded in thought and structure by ten or twenty other lines. Perhaps it is embedded in the middle, or perhaps it is not even a line, but two half lines. Sometimes it epitomizes a thought so pregnantly that it is the line I must lead off with, and build up from.

Then comes a third stage, once the rough structure is built, once something is put down, the work of polishing and discarding begins. In the rough structure, in order to get a framework at all costs, I will have left blanks, left out rhymes, left out even whole

Note—This chapter is from diaries and letters by the author.

73

lines. In this third stage I can safely go back and change words, switch lines back and forth, try them here and there, for now I have something to work on and manipulate mentally. At least some of the "silver eels of thought" as Virginia Woolf calls them have been captured in the net.

For example, the first draft of "You have known beauty of a different kind" is a series of illegible words and phrases which were the product of a desire to set these words on paper. In the second attempt, what seems to be emerging is a contrast between two kinds of beauty, belonging to two different people.

> You have known Beauty of a different kind
> From that which radiates and floods my soul
> You have . . . . . visions . . . . different goal
> The unrelenting structure . . . . . of the mind
> From those which captivate my heart and mind
> The bare and unrelenting structure
> Slender grey . . . . . . held in niche of stone
> The gothic arches moonlit and austere
> Earth's unrelenting structure of conceptual thought
> Give you their secrets
> rendering to its own.
>
> From those which flash bright colors through my mind
>
> Earth's fundamental structure . . . . . . and clear
> Claims your allegiance, rendering you its own
> Has claimed your being, rendering you its own
> Gold, gothic arches, moonlit and austere
> Designs of abstract thought

In the third attempt, what is dealt with is an accentuation of the contrast between the two worlds.

> I walk a stranger in your world.
>
> To light a candle with my singing praise
> You have known Beauty of a different kind
> From that which radiates and floods my soul

You have sensed visions of another goal
From those which flash bright colors through my mind.

I walk a pilgrim from another land
In this cathedral hush, Dim lights . . . . .
I cannot even see, bare headed stand

Alone invites these . . . . . diverse
The form and color of the Universe.

The final, published version runs:

You have known Beauty of a different kind
From that which radiates and floods my soul.
You have had visions of a different goal
From that which stabs its colors through my mind.
Earth's fundamental structure, sharp and clear
Claims your allegiance. Yielding up its own
Design to abstract thought; cold and austere
Its gothic arches rise in silvered stone.
I walk, a pilgrim from another land
In this cathedral. Vaulted roof above
I only dimly see. But as I stand
And light my candle at the shrine of love
I bind in flame these attributes diverse . . .
The form and color of the Universe.

These observations find interesting echoes in Melville Cane's work. Apropos of rough draft, he writes:

. . . This is a moment of danger, when in a fit of disgust and self-mortification the poet is liable to tear up what he has done as worthless. It is important not to succumb to this mood of despair since one is in no condition to evaluate whatever he may have accomplished up to this point.

Therefore one should salvage those trial sheets from the waste paper basket and keep them available so that they may be reconsidered at some later time. You'll often find, to your agreeable surprise, that your original impulse was sound and capable of further successful development.

He is also concerned with the "mysterious urge" and has had an identical experience of a single phrase "demanding" to be placed in a certain position in a poem. Melville Cane writes the following:

> I would like to stress the need for awareness and vigilance at the instant when one first feels the *mysterious summons* of the creative current. (1)

> The initial haunting phrase struck me as the *right unit line to set the pace* and suggest the climate of the poem. (1)

A more recent observation on what triggers a poem is the following:

When mood and external happening bear certain psychophysiological similarities, or use Koffka's phrase, when the "inner and outer environment coincide," (10) this particular constellation of events allows a poem to be triggered.

In the following poem, the potentially arid mood of the observer is exorcised by the recognition of the common element between the mood and the desert.

> Though you entice me
> With the scintillating gold
> Of your evening skies
>   I will not gamble with my affection
>
> Though you spread before me
> The purple plush
> Of your sunset hills
> You cannot lure me to love you.
>
> Though you scatter over the black firmament
> The diamond stars
> Of your jewelry
> You cannot evoke my desire to possess you.
>
> For as I look closer
> I see your face
> And you are old, and scarred and ugly

Below your painted perfection
I see your arid wrinkles
I see the sharp and vicious nails
On your destructive, cactus hands
And as I probe your deception
Violently you spew upon me
The suffocating dust of your hot and angry breath.

The relationship between mood and environmental characteristics or atmosphere is obviously not simple. One and the same physical environment can call out different feelings in the same person at different times, to say nothing of different feelings in two people at the same time. Yet there seem to be some limiting conditions.

A mood of oppression may have existed for some time, with the poet passing through many environmental settings. Suddenly the "appropriate" stimulus allows verbalization and release. What constitues "appropriate" is, of course, the crux of the matter.

A small room, used as a library which has been a cozy work setting for years, may suddenly become confining and prison-like, as in "Nightmare."

Bricked up with books
Entombed alive, stiffled
By non-essentials that stultify living.

Bulldose the ediface
Let intellectual-status be riffled
Break through for air, for movement and for giving.

Regardless of the inner pressure, however, not just any externalization will serve. It would be impossible, for instance, for the awesome experience of the gigantic monolith, Stone Mountain, to evoke the claustrophobic "Nightmare" lines; conversely a library could not have triggered the preoccupation with psychological and geological stoniness, expressed in the following poem:

STONE MOUNTAIN

Yesterday
In unproductive fantasy
I had hung a mill-stone round my neck
I had given mine adversary a heart of stone.

Thus I no longer moved with accustomed swiftness
Nor opened myself to others.

Today
The stone, the mountainous stone
Is anchored, where it belongs
In neutral, timeless, impersonal grandeur
And I am free.

In somewhat the same way the visual pattern of a poem, the shape it is to have on the page, may be described by certain key words, as for example in "Crisis," the opposition of *stark* and *diffusion*.

CRISIS

Lightening
Stark
Blinding
Throwing into bold relief
Only meaningful patterns
Etching only crucial values
On eternity.

Hold this perspective
When, unexpectedly returns
The soft, permissive, diffusing, confusing
Reassuring, blurring light of routine day.

Chapter IX

THE SELF-SUSTAINING POEMS

IN NOTES AND LETTERS written at this time (1950) the idea of the self-sustaining features of poems emerges.

> I now see the writing of poems as a self-regulatory function acting as a counterbalance both to over-elation and depression. It would seem as if the pressure necessary for writing may be positive or negative. The positive pressure is one of potentially ungovernable excitement, the negative is that vector towards depression, the feeling of loss, or the feeling of being abandoned and rejected. It seems that the poems I write as a result of this negative pressure constitute reassurances that this loss is less vital than what has already been gained. The poem attempts to arrest depression, not by ignoring it or attempting to cover it up, but by giving it in itself a place in a more positive picture.

In terms of one's own development, this need to *give* the poem is still important, but it must reach out to a wider audience. Psychological health is, in the last analysis, a matter of how we relate to others. No restoring or sustaining process can occur if it does not relate one in some new way to another person. Thus the ebullient, pressureful, manic-like poems have as their very essence the communication of at all costs the potentially unwieldy mass of feeling.

To be communicated this feeling must become intelligible, and

Note—The poems in this chapter are taken from *Time to Squander, Time to Reap*, New Bedford, Reynolds DeWalt Printing, 1946 and 1965.

to become intelligible it must lose its unstructured, completely egocentric aspect. What we might call, then, the "warding-off-depression" poems demand communication because they have become a triumphant rather than a defeatist gesture. They seem to say I am not alone if it is known that I can stand being alone.

These antidepression poems seem to insist on a positive acceptance of what is, because by so doing they protect a precious experience from a damage that might come to it by retroactive depressive trends.

Melville Cane again expresses many similar ideas. He writes of the need to share a poem, and the need to utilize or convert "emotional shock from its negative content to something positive and constructive." He further states:

> Since the act of creation is two-fold, an offering and a response, the poet cannot be satisfied with merely pleasing himself. If that were all, he would not need to be understood by anyone but himself; he could indulge his fancies at will for his purely private consumption. The poet fails, when he fails to communicate.

Elsewhere in the same chapter he speaks of being sufficiently detached:

> . . . . to realize that here at hand was an unexpected gift of creative energy which I must not reject, but must put to positive advantage. To state it in another way, I was driven consciously to convert this emotional shock from its negative content to something positive and constructive. Should I succeed in this effort at self control I would psychologically do myself a service and in the process conceivably achieve a poem. The kind of poem I might produce, its subject, its mood, was, of course, unpredictable.

The poems in this chapter have been chosen, then, to illustrate this contention that one of the functions of poetry is to restore an inner balance that has temporarily been lost. The writing of the poem seems to provide comfort when external solace is lacking. The poem reactivates memories or experiences which have given meaning and value to life.

This is not done with conscious motivation at the time. Yet, looking back many years later at poems written during times of stress, loneliness and sadness, it is possible to detect these self-therapeutic trends.

As a result of the reactivation of memory and meaningful moments, the vulnerable part of the self is able to shift the psychic point of departure. Loneliness or despair are no longer the paramount feelings, rather there is a challenge to "recapture heights." Thus a period of potentially stagnating depression may be averted, and the individual reoriented to more positive goals.

Poems may bring back into sharp focus a loved one who has been lost.

> May it bring gladness to you that you made
> Of me no follower, disciple, slave,
> No weakling, leaning on the love you gave
> As prop and pillar. Rather the bright blade
> That lay at my own feet you did restore
> To my right hand. Your torch rekindled mine,
> So that from eyes unclouded now may shine
> That fierce crusader's faith I knew of yore.
> Henceforward must the song of all I do
> In all its parts harmonious be in tone.
> But one design shall guide me through and through,
> Chiselled from but one selfsame block of stone
> What mind and heart desire. Thus losing you
> I yet recapture heights I once have known.

> I have protested. I have fought with fate.
> I have refused to bow to time's decree,
> To reason's ruse, or the conspiracy
> Of distant lands and sea to separate
> My life from yours, my thinking from your thought,
> My loving from your love, pride from your pride
> That to eternal values, side by side,
> We might pay tribute—offerings love had wrought.
> My feeble protests, what have they availed?
> I've lost each round, I've failed at every turn.

My adversaries won, with much to spare.
And now Death's ultimatum has prevailed.
Yet just as long as longing's flame can burn
I walk the mountain path, and you are there!

If I must say goodbye to you, it shall be this:
"You who command
In me that surge of tenderness and power,
You, whose dear hand
Captures eternity within an hour,
There is no parting of the ways for us.
For though the days of sadness take their toll
Sapping the strength,
And even that rare freedom of the soul
That is my life with you, I may not keep;
Yet I have known a life that is a whole
Where joy and sorrow blended in the deep
Immeasurable meaning that is you.
Goodbye, for in goodbye I also say
For us there is no parting of the way."

In a less traditional poetic form, the subsequent poem may be considered an example of the same underlying need.

Be very still my heart
Do not confuse
Bravery with busy-ness.

For it is not virtuous
To smother longing
Under a pile of deeds
Nor to drag intellectual furniture
Into the empty rooms of the mind
To fill the void.

The void cannot be filled:
The loved one is not there.

Rather
Savour this emptiness.
Give it full scope.
For it is the inevitable counterpart,
The just and delicate balance
Of fulfilled love and devotion.

Live within this emptiness
For here, the vulnerable and dilated self
May re-define its own boundaries
May set its own pace
May again find its own peace

Therefore, be still my heart
          and be very grateful.

It is not only the loss of a loved person that triggers depression, nor are the only conflicts experienced those directly connected with other persons. One of the most effective uses of poetry from the self-therapeutic point of view is the opportunity it affords to objectify any hampering experience. Objectifying brings about externalization and the poet is no longer sunk in the emotional morass.

The poems which follow have been directed towards a variety of devitalizing experiences. Two sonnets, for instance, attempt to keep obsessional thoughts at bay and handle mounting and shattering inner tension.

There is a vacuum created when the mind
Will of a sudden cease its arduous tasks.
Then as an angry mob that no one asks
To enter, breaks all barriers; or as wind
Will howl and rush down through a canyon'd street
As monstrous tidal wave, or thunder's roar
Will fill the gap that nature does abhor,
So do my thoughts with wild insistence beat,
To splinters shattering will's fragile door,
Breaking the locks of resolution's setting,
Crumbling the walls built to enforce forgetting,
Levelling the props that pride has raised before.

Should my mind rest one minute of the hour,
Tornado-like these thoughts will show their power.

There was a time when all my life was held
Between two poles, with ever mounting tension
Of nerve and heart, as if some great suspension
Bridge that spans a chasm were compelled
To a mad death-dance of annihilation,
Locked in the clutches of some one vibration.
Doomed despite planning and its pliant steel,
Doomed despite all the care of its construction,
Doomed despite all its service to destruction.
And at that time when all my heart could feel
Was frenzied longing, when my mind could live
Only in terms of you and what you give,
I might have fallen. But that time is past;
I am at peace within myself at last.

Feelings of guilt or failure to live close to an ideal may also
absorb energy. The three poems which follow demonstrate first,
the recognition of this failure, then an attempt to resolve the con-
flict which was producing the feelings of guilt, and finally an ex-
pression of rebirth. I cannot stress too strongly the fact that at the
time of writing none of this kind of "editorial awareness" was pres-
ent. The poems spring from acute feelings which must be handled,
and the self-therapeutic purpose is completely hidden to the
writer at the time.

They are whirling against my mind
These thoughts, like giant snow-flakes,
And their maddening flurry
Blinds my eyes
And has cut short my breath.

They are driving against my mind
As fierce as hail-stones,
These thoughts that burn me

With their accusation:
For I have come down from the heights
And have become mortal
Growing afraid to stand alone
Where he must stand
Who holds in trust the holy grail of truth.

I can walk once more on the high places.
Strong wind and fierce sun are my friends;
Steep mountain paths my spirit retraces,
And its long vigil ends.

I can walk once more on the high places,
And to him that would have it, bequeath
The luxuriant earth, and the life it embraces
In the lush vale beneath.

How can I make these words sound like a bell,
A slow and solemn bell? It does not toll
For sorrow, but it is the passing knell
Of compromise, of bartering the soul
For grease, that custom's chariot wheels may roll.

What wings of gladness can I give these words?
Shall I take silver flute, or golden horn,
Beethovens' song of Joy, tumultuous birds
A-clatter and a-clamour on May mour?
Deluged in song, this day I am reborn.

In the next two poems there seems to be an attempt to shake
loose from a miasmic sadness. While this is not so dramatic as is
the battling with obsessional thoughts, and not so disturbing or
powerful as feelings of guilt, nonetheless it is a hampering and
devitalizing experience in the sense that the efficacy of the total
organism is unquestionably diminished.

Dull heart of mine,
Here's sparkling wine
Of rich September,
Must moods of May
Always hold sway?
Must you remember?

When sumacs shout
And all about
Bustles the Fall,
The dreamy haze
Of soft June days
Must you recall?

When white-capped sea
And flaming tree
Give their own rapture,
Indolent sky
Of lush July
Must you recapture?

Slow heart of mine,
Must you still pine
For August golden?
Find swift delight
In woodland bright,
Let winds embolden.

Too constant heart,
Awake and start
New work, new pleasure.
Time cannot steal,
Blur nor repeal,
Your summer's treasure.

November mists, my heart's November moods!
Uncertain hybrid month
Afraid to take your stand,
Loath to remember

Your duties as the herald of December,
Loath to be prologue to the tragic acts
Winter will shortly play,
You temporize each day,
You vacillate
You recreate
A still soft summer noon.
You hesitate,
You imitate
October's harvest moon.
The summer's weeds
Silvered in your pale sun,
Blue smoke from burning leaves,
The drypoint etching of black trees—
See! these
Are your procrastinating substitutes for all
The frank, full blooded brilliance of the fall.
Come, take your stand,
Play your appointed role,
Proclaim with frosty breath the naked truth:
Gone are the golden days of love and youth.

All writers and poets are plagued at times with the experience of being blocked, unable to write, unable to get started, unable to believe in the fact that their productions have the slightest value. The recognition of certain components in the blocking, via the medium of verse, can bring about release of energy that is temporarily out of commission and unavailable for creative use.

Heart that's too proud
To cry aloud,
Or show
Its tears at mortal blow,
What shall it gain?
How shall it grow?
The heart with busy business sign
On bankrupt shop,
The heart with clownish pantomime
Till curtain-drop,
The heart too vain

> To bow to pain,
> Or meet
> Steadfast, defeat,
> What shall it gain?
> How shall it grow?

Uncertainty is an emotional experience which can undermine the strongest psyche. When the inner universe is engulfed by uncertainty, we find the poet struggling to establish the minimum security required for existence, and speaking of fear:

> Fear is night and blackness
> It is endless emptiness
> It is floodless and wall-less
> It lacks the horizontal and the perpendicular
> There is no gravity
> No solid substance to manipulate

At a lessor degree uncertainty seems to be able to be captured and pinned down in a short verse of different intensity:

> Uncertainty!
> Mind's pendulum first moves
> Between uneasiness and pleasure
> In well-appointed grooves—
> No great catastrophe, no great treasure.

> Uncertainty!
> Pendulum further swings,
> Joy touches heart, fear clutches heart,
> Each oscillation brings
> Added momentum, and its counterpart
> Added uncertainty.

> Uncertainty!
> Pendulum swings wide,
> Rackets from side to side,
> Despair, ecstasy, left, right,
> Hope vanishes, triumph in sight,
> Goals shattered, goals attained,
> Ideas mud-spattered, goals attained,
> Agonizing, vitalizing
> Uncertainty!

The poetic antennae sometimes will pick up a mood which is nameless, too slight or fleeting to be dignified by a label or title, yet experienced in all its subtlety. Thus the feeling of not being one's complete self in some encounters is nicely caught in this:

House cleaned for party!
Immaculate, impersonal, austere,
(I live here?)
Fresh paint
On woodwork and casement;
Dogs perplexed
At new restraint
Retire to basement.
Children vexed,
Ordered to pick up toys
And stop noise,
Cook taxed
To point of screaming,
But cauldrons steaming,
Silver gleaming
And glasses crystal clear.
(I live here?
Where are the things I need,
The books I use,
Pen, papers, letters,
Comfortable old shoes?)

The threatening passage of time is somewhat mollified by the reversal of the process in fantasy, in that the gift of a watch has become the gift of time.

You leave me Time! And symbol though it be
What greater gift could even God bestow?
Time: that insurgent and tumultous thoughts may grow
Through adolescence to maturity.
Time: that my love, holding in one fierce flame
Its full potential, nonetheless may trace
A living pattern, which will weave your name
Into the very substance of my days.
You leave me Time; from the Unconscious sea
In which we cast our nets, and not in vain,

You draw the symbol to replenish me
You catch the symbol to annul the pain
Of parting. Time is not empty, Time is to recapture
The whirlwind, and the calm that follows, rapture.

The self-sustaining aspect of poetry could also be seen as part of the individual's struggle to achieve or maintain his personal integrity. In this connection Erikson's description of the mature individual's need to defend the dignity of his own life style is pertinent (Italics mine):

Only he who in some way has taken care of things and people and has adapted himself to the triumphs and disappointments adherent to being, by necessity, the originator of others and the generator of things and ideas—only he may gradually grow the fruit of the seven stages. I know no better word for it than *integrity*. *Lacking a clear definition, I shall point to a few attributes of this state of mind. It is the acceptance of one's one-and-only life cycle and of the people who have become significant to it as something that had to be and that, by necessity, permitted of no substitutions.* It thus means a new, a different love of one's parents, free of the wish that they should have been different, and an acceptance of the fact that one's life is one's own responsibility. It is a sense of comradeship with men and women of distant times and of different pursuits, who have created orders and objects and sayings conveying human dignity and love. *Although aware of the relativity of all the various life styles which have given meaning to human striving, the possessor of integrity is ready to defend the dignity of his own life style against all physical and economic threats.* For he knows that an individual life is the accidental coincidence of but one life cycle with but one segment of history; and that for him all human integrity stands or falls with the one style of integrity of which he partakes.

This, then, is a beginning for a formulation of integrity based on my experience in clinical and anthropological fields: it is here, above all else, where each reader, each discussant, each group, must continue to develop in his or its own terms what I have gropingly begun in mine. But I can add, clinically, *that the lack or loss of this accrued ego integration is signified by an often unconscious fear of death and despair: the one and only life cycle is not accepted as the ultimate of life.* Despair expresses the feeling that the time is short, too short for the attempt to start another life and to try out alternate roads to integrity. Such a despair is often hidden behind a show of disgust, a misanthropy, or a chronic contemptuous displeasure with particular institutions and particular people—a disgust and a displeasure which (where not allied with constructive ideas and a life of cooperation) only signify the individual's contempt for himself. (2, p. 143)

The writing of poems is an integral part of the individual's struggle to achieve this integrity. Poems are written during personal crises; they are not written with the *explicit* wish to triumph over adversity, yet, in their execution and achievement they reaffirm the "dignity of the life style." Once achieved, they consolidate the position, reinforce the ground gained against despair and meaninglessness.

Finally, creating the poem may serve to mitigate against the poet's awareness of the high cost of being alive and of his own finiteness.

> I must pay a price for your presence
> For closeness to you has sharpened
> That terrifying knife-blade knowledge
> That this span of awareness
> That is me, that is mine,
> Is finite.
>
> I must pay a price for your presence
> Without you, ostrich-like
> I can bury my head, can disregard the nagging query
> How, once vouchsafed consciousness,
> Can a being die?
>
> I must pay a price for your presence
> Without you I can forget
> That this second by second
> Opportunity
> To sense, to feel, to know, to love
> This cherished awesome awareness
> Must sometime end.
>
> I must pay a price for your presence
> With the sober recognition

That even the pinnacle of evolution
This fusion of consciousness
This bridging the gap between two personal worlds
Will also cease.

Sensing this poignant passing with each breath
I pay the price and strive for peace with death.

Chapter X

THE POET-SELF SEARCHES AGAIN

POEMS WRITTEN during the search for greater self-knowledge, the therapeutic experience, seem to have several main functions. Some poems may be thought of as signposts indicating the direction in which the individual wishes to move in subsequent sessions. It is easier, for example, for some creative persons and certainly for our poet, to approach the area of positive transference by way of a poem rather than by recounting a dream.

Such poems may be indirect or direct. The poem entitled "Telephone" is an example of one written ostensibly around the reaction of an individual to a telephone call in general, but was, of course, when associated to, seen as prompted by a call from the therapist.

TELEPHONE

Like a stone
Into a quiet pond
Of studious consciousness
Comes your voice!
And the pond is a-shimmer
With ripples
A-glimmer with dancing light.

Like a shot
At dusk in the forest

Note—This chapter is adapted from Molly Harrower, Poems emerging from the therapeutic experience, *Journal of Mental Disorders*, Vol. 149, pp. 213–233, 1969.

Comes your voice
And the myriad birds of thought
Break into the air with wild cries
Wheeling and swooping in disarray
Their ranks disbanded,
And orderly contemplation is shattered
In the excited whirr of wings.

Like a comet
Splintering the austere heavens
Of the mind absorbed,
Comes your voice.
And the sky grows luminous
With the pulse of numberless stars
Now tumultous and exultant.

Another example is a poem concerning the perilous isolation engendered by a missed appointment. Such an experience can be better communicated by verse than by prose and is a stepping-stone towards the communication of feelings, the growing need of the patient for the analyst's support.

I am held
Within an invisible framework,
Within a field of force
Which batters the idea-particles
Which galvanizes the image-filings
Till they leap to the magnet of the solution.
NO APPOINTMENT
I am suspended
In sparseness
In a Wasteland
In a Dali desert,
There are canyons of consciousness
Uncrossed by cables of communication
I am alone.

A more overt explicit acknowledgment of the need for the therapist and his importance in the patient's life is seen in the following:

TRANSFERENCE NEUROSIS

You give me the spring morning
The dogwood and peachblossom
Framed in the window—which you have opened

But I, who long have known
That only at such a casement
Could I sing, and sing freely
I, now have no voice.

You give me a sense of companionship
Such that solitude is never isolation,
So that Time is a garden
And against the white wall of my contentment
The moments I hold precious
Like flaming peonies
Burst with a splash, and a splash of splendour.

But I, who would show this to you
In the paint of words
Now find the pallet of my imagery
Dry and dirty.

You, by what finite means I shall never discover
Fill me with infinite joy,
And that joy is a light
And that light is a beacon
In the darkness of others who are bewildered.

But I, who would come into your presence
Caught in the beam of its brilliance
Am blinded and step out into the shadows,
So that you never see me—as I can stand,—
Held in a radiance that is jointly of your making.

Some poems are concerned with elaborating, in afterthought,
a phrase of the therapist's. In the role of psychologist-therapist
(that is, when functioning in my nonpoet professional role), I
have frequently been struck by the fact that the phrases which

seem to be so challenging and meaningful to a patient are rarely those which I have felt to be particularly meaningful ones. Be that as it may, in the following illustration this poet seems to have been challenged by the question "Are you a person without echos?"

A person without echos!
God forbid!
As if the past ceased to reverberate
As if the past ceased to color, to impregnate and to re-enforce
Each living moment.

A person without echos!
Thin and trite
A shadow shifting ceaselessly
Devoid of roots, responsibility
For its own presence.

A person without echos: No,
For me the past is more than echos.
It is a lively orchestra
It is a solid platform to stand on
It is built with love and sweat and tears
And hammered fingers.

The echos from the past include discarded fantasies.
In the echos from the past there is the whirr and sifting of emotion's
    wheat and chaff
The sifting required for finer and finer scrutiny
Of the so-called eternal verities until only the immutable remains.

And such a past
Gives joy, warmth and security
When it is called on as the backdrop
For an act of love.

Another example of a single phrase associated to or blended into verse is the therapist's "Why so angry?"

    This isn't anger—or perhaps it is,
    Anger is a word, but I am still living this

It is running through me, I am swimming in it
There is a match in my pocket
I am breaking it into small pieces
I am cornered, at bay, trapped
I am a boxer without hands
A poet with aphasia.
There is somewhere a great Unfairness
Something is Unfair, how to catch it, how to show it?

I have been cornered, outmaneuvered
I have no weapons to fight this phase of the battle
Outmaneuvered: cornered: it's the old nursery anguish
The reasoning of the all-powerful Grown-Ups
The omnipotent grown-ups who can enforce,
Who can withhold
Who can blight, who can ruin.
Grown-Ups who do things for "ones good"
Who take the dog away
Because it isn't good for one to sleep with the dog
The dog is life and warmth and happiness
What can there be that is good for one without that?

It is the crazy reasoning of the all-powerful Teachers
You must not walk with your friend
Because she is your friend
Therefore you must walk with another little girl
Who is not your friend, because it is good for you
What is good for you except your friend!
But the Grown-ups hold the power, there is nothing one can do
There is only the sense of burning injustice
And he who asks that question holds the power.

Using a somewhat different poetic idiom, the poet reacted at times with a flow of semi-serious verse. The discussion had centered around the poet's vulnerability in certain situations and the therapist had mentioned some form of avoiding, or blocking out, the most intense and hurtful experiences that resulted from oversensitivity. Somehow the metaphor of installing a "shutter" had been mentioned and the poet reacted against this and was then able to formulate a personal orientation to some of life's problems.

I confided to my boat
As I sat there bailing
"Now the wind's freshening
And the sky's so blue
And the time's just ripe
For us to go a-sailing,
How should I get a shutter
Like I promised to?"

My boat tossed her jib
And stamped with her boom
"I don't like your sentiments
They're petty and they're small
You'll sail with pennant flying
With your heart alive and crying
With the very joy of living
If you sail with me at all."

So I then asked the stars
As I slept beneath the heavens
"Lamps of Eternity
You must know my mind.
I'm supposed to shut it off
From the light of love and longing
Can you tell me where to get
A shutter or a blind?"

But my very simple question
Made 'em all uproar'ous
Two stars went a-shooting
And a meteor blazed
"Dear little simpleton"
They all proclaimed in chorus
"We don't deal in shutters
The Lord be praised."

So I said to my heart
"Must I go on searching
To find those opiates
That they say will give you peace?
Do you want to be embalmed,

Protected, barricaded?
Will you really *be* contented
When your longings cease?

"All this talk" said my heart,
"Makes me furious.
I don't like shutters
And I won't be supplied
The only blinds I'll draw
Are to keep from the curious
The beauty and the brilliance
Of the light inside."

Equally lighthearted, but nonetheless a struggle with the same basic problem, and triggered by the same words of the therapists, is the following:

ADVICE TO MYSELF ON INSTALLING A SHUTTER

On household tasks exhausting
(Which you always think are frightful)
You must enter with a flourish,
Find the dishes quite delightful
Find the ordering a pleasure
For of course the price of butter
Contributes beyond measure
T'wards installing of a shutter.

Yes, remember the essentials
As around the house you putter
Keep your mind encased in blinkers
You're developing a shutter.

When you're busy entertaining
Every John and Jane and Harry
Who bore you to extinction
And who always seem to tarry
When your thoughts go drifting elsewhere
(To that man you cannot marry)
You must pull yourself up shortly
Such intrusions you must parry.

And remember the essentials
As you dutifully stutter
"O won't you stay to dinner"
You're developing a shutter

In matters scientific
There is apt to be a skutter
For trains of thought short-circuit
And confusion may be utter
You may think that you're objective
When you study dreams and Freud
But probably you're doing
Just the thing you should avoid.

For since all roads lead to Rome
You must recognize the cues
That are leading you astray
If shutters you will use.

As you stagger to your bedroom
After many hours of toiling
To install this silly shutter
And your temper it is boiling
You can drop responsibility
As sleepily you mutter
"Now the censor can take over
And can regulate the shutter"

And if the censor's napping
Then you're obviously blameless
You can wander through your dreams
Quite shutterless and shameless!

Some peculiarly poignant moments in therapy are reacted to by lyrical outbursts as in the case of the poems entitled "Insight" and "I am so Happy That I Burn the People who Pass Me."

INSIGHT

I feel like a tree in which the sap
Is suddenly flowing freely.

Not a young tree with buds,
But a tree that is bearing fruit.
I feel the quintescence of aliveness.
I feel power: the new element which makes all else seem new.

I feel like a series of explosions
Held together on a base of profound peace.
My mind is going off like a fire cracker
But my heart knows an equilibrium,
A stability, a contentment
That is richer than anything the earth has yet given me

The most exciting thoughts are the new-old ones
Based on previous idea-adventures
But re-stated, with a sharp new angle
Thrown into focus
Re-emphasised, re-phrased
The same, yet deeper and more penetrating.

Freedom, love and laughter
These were all mine
Since I could think and feel
But I have reached them by a new path
They are old friends, old values
But they come back to me clean and new
With accumulated scum seared off them by acid
Deloused of sentimentality.

I AM SO HAPPY . . .

I am so happy that I burn the people who pass me
Particularly those who have also known ecstasy
And are on good terms with laughter.
But even the people who live on the shady side of the street,
The people who pull down the curtains on life
The people who cover the parlor carpet with newspaper
In case it should fade . . .
Even they look up as I pass, and say
"Why, the sun is pleasant this morning . . . quite springlike."

A poem like the "Five Freedoms," a dialogue between two selves, is obviously the summation of many sessions and reflects the patient's deep-seated feelings of release in various areas. Freedom of thought, freedom to love, freedom from guilt, freedom from fear and freedom for happiness.

Five Freedoms: Five new Universes
In which to live and move and have one's being.

FREEDOM OF THOUGHT:

"But that's banal
I'm a good democrat and a good liberal
This is a free country and I think as I please!"

"But *how* do you please? Can you hold a constant course
Can you keep out the vagrant hoard of irrelevant fantasies?
Can you discard the strait-jacket of habit?
Or lose for an instant, hounded by an idea,
That shadow-follower obsession?
Are you free to think when you please?
Have you not lived through hours of tense tedium
Because, by no possible effort of will,
Can you establish a connection
Between brain-burden and point of poised pencil?
Have you not lived through nights
When thoughts, like vicious jockeys
Rode *you* to death on a circular course?
Freedom of thought: a new Universe."

FREEDOM TO LOVE:

"I have loved as I chose
I have been free. There you cannot taunt me,
I have defied convention, I have . . ."

"Is that a fact?
Then you have at all times demanded as your birthright
The fierce gladness of the body's rapture?
You have never argued, to stifle sickening disappointment,
That perhaps, after all, 'They' were right
That perhaps, after all, you had demanded too much of life . . . ?
You have never turned aside in sadness
Because, for this or that, for him or her, you must renounce
That which, for very longing of it, was your due,
That which, because you could envisage it, was yours?
You have never compromised?
You have never accepted as full nourishment
Scraps you would have scorned to offer to a beggar?
You are sure?
Freedom to love; a new Universe."

FREEDOM FROM FEAR:

"Now that's just plain funny
Sure, I've been nervous, but it adds zip to life.
Stage fright, huge crowds, and better performance,
Tautness on the high dive
Tension as the horse comes to the jump
Skipped heart-beat as ski slips on fast slope,
Scared before examination or big interview
And one comes out tops."

"That's not fear.
Fear is night and blackness
It is endless emptiness
It is floorless and wall-less
It lacks the horizontal and the perpendicular
There is no gravity
There is no point of light for direction
No solid substance to manipulate
No sound, no echo
No single hold to which the amorphous organism
Can cling to prevent its dissolution."

"That . . . . . that was insanity . . . . ."
                                        "No, fear.
Freedom from fear: a new Universe."

FREEDOM FROM GUILT:

                    "But I feel guiltless
Ashamed of nothing, nothing to be ashamed of . . .
I claim, with Wilde, that to regret ones past
Is to deny ones identity."

"I know that feeling well. But let me ask you
What court has scrutinized your actions?"

"Myself, I am sole judge, what do you think
That I am tied to my mother's apron strings?"

"Of course, of course, you outgrew tedious morals long ago,
Shook off the nurse maid, and the Sunday school.
Its as you say, you are sole judge,
But let me suggest one slight modification—
Bring along another judge to court with you."

"Who?"

"O well, some friend or colleague
Let him sit beside you on the bench. . . . ."

"But he would interrupt me . . ."

"No, he'd only listen."

"But he would over-rule my decisions . . .
He would question my authority . . .
He would make me feel . . ."

"Whats the matter? Who said he would be judging YOU?
Freedom from guilt: a new Universe."

FREEDOM FOR HAPPINESS:

> *"But I have been happy.*
> *Why! I remember when I was a child*
> *The Grown-Ups used to say*
> *Is the sun shining?*
> *No it's only the little girl who always laughs"*

"Granted you have a goodly heritage
But have you guarded that happiness?
Did you openly acknowledge it as more precious
Than life itself?
Did you know that Duty, dressed in black crepe
Handcuffed to self-conscious virtue
Was only a travesty?
Did you know that joy was a creation
A work of art
An achievement?"

"An achievement? Why no,
For many said that I had been born
With a silver spoon in my mouth,
Or that I had had more than my share.
Others made me feel that happiness was selfishness
That laughter could never enter the holy of holies,
That life was a responsibility . . ."

"*Happiness* is the responsibility!
It is an inward barometer
Of the well being of body and mind
And their inter-relation.
It is a precise indicator, a balance
Exact and intricate
Reflecting interaction and timing of ever changing needs and desires
It is an exquisite, a fantastically delicate instrument,
To be treasured
To be lived by
With full realization of every minute of fulfillment,
Exultantly and without apology."

Poems may be used to express a deepened insight into or aware-
ness of a psychophysical parallelism or a psychosomatic malfunc-

tion of conflict. This poem, entitled "Visceral Spasm," is a good
example:

> Danger, malfunction
> Disruption of the established order
> Stoppage—jolt—jar—
> Monkey-wrench thrown—
> Sudden awareness
> Where no awareness existed
> Shattered and broken patterns
> Abrupt end to inward rhythm
> And relaxed periodicity.
>
> Sound the alarm in two languages
> Diverse in grammar and syntax
> But with common intonation and phrasing
> Sound the alarm in the language of muscle and blood
> Of cramp and spasm
> Of tortured tissue
> Revolting against alien invaders
>
> Sound the alarm in the language of consciousness
> In the language of pain and tension
> Of uneasiness, irritability and restlessness.
>
> And in this dual, isomorphic, outcry
> Let the organism protest,
> Clamor and demand
> Its right to the full harmony of living.

Sooner or later, in the therapeutic experience, women, poets in-
cluded, struggle with their feelings of ambivalence in regard to
domesticity on the one hand and their careers or ego-enhancing
activities on the other.

Freedom is longed for, striven for, but then frequently is found
wanting. Here is one such ambivalent mood in a lighter vein:

OF WHAT AVAIL ART THOU, FREEDOM?

> Free to take a long vacation
> Unencumbered, coast to coast,

Free to oscillate and shuttle
Playfully from ghost to ghost.
Free to cast a roving eyeball
On enamored swains, a host,
Free to spend the morning reading
Time or Life or Evening Post.

But what do these things avail me?
Of essentials I can't boast.
Now anxieties assail me
And with fears I am engrossed.
Though there ain't no Summum Bonum
Chores for Menfolk *Do* count most.

There is also the struggle with the question of concentration or
diffusion, with dedication or with free love, in their amorous mo-
ments. The following poem epitomizes the emergence from an
essentially child-like attitude to what might be described as the
growing pains of discarding parental disapproval to greater ma-
turity.

There is no sin
For me but this
That I should win
A minor bliss
That I begin
And end amiss
There is no sin
To me but this.
To take a kiss
To please the skin
And be within
My heart amiss
There is no sin
To me but this.

To me it's sin
I must confess
If all within
My heart says yes

> Yet Custom's din
> Will cause me stress
> To me it's sin
> I must confess
> If fear's duress
> Should hold within
> Me, words which bless
> Which you should win
> To me that's sin
> I must confess.
>
> To me the sin
> I frankly state
> Is, if within
> My heart you rate
> As closest kin
> Yet still to wait
> To me that's sin
> I frankly state.
> If to donate
> What you should win
> When mind's akin
> I'm tardy, late
> To me that's sin
> I frankly state.

Again, in this new searching period, we find the poet struggling with the apparent collapse of the ideas and concepts which have been standbys in the preceding years. And, just as for the adolescent, the poem gave a reassurance in the midst of chaos, so we find a recurrence of the use of poems in this way.

> It has become fashionable
> To discard the word Value
> To build new concepts to displace it.
>
> It has become fashionable
> To recognize the reciprocity
> Of needs and hungers
> Which underlie all relationships.

It has become fashionable
To beware of over-valuing the desired object
And it is naive blundering
To be concerned with love when sex explains it better.

It has become fashionable but to what avail?
For Beauty still overpowers
And love does have a vector which carries beyond the self
Love has directed-ness
It is a circuit action simple, basic and fundamental.
The shortest route between points A and B
Or between thee and me.

The same kind of thought may be seen in these few lines:

> When you abandon love
> Dig a dirt hollow, six feet
> Unceremoniously bury
> Scorching the earth in retreat
>
> Some day from fireblackened sod
> May spring a wild cherry.

Or again in a similar vein:

> And if no more than this—still gratitude
> If all hopes are illusory
> All systems of value outmoded
> All intellectual concepts inadequate
> If love is but the expression of need
> If desire to combat violence
> If the loathing of cruelty
> Is but the mirror image
> Of repressed sadistic trends—still gratitude
> That this illusion has been faced.

An important part of many therapeutic experiences, the guided exploration of the searching self, is coming to terms with dependent needs. To what extent have love relationships been unsatisfactory for a women because she has not been able to experience genuine submission? Particularly in a world which permits so many women to assume legitimate and dominant roles in their professional fields, there is danger that this basic component of submitting to mastery may have been lost or never experienced.

My emotional diet has lacked an important ingredient all these years.
My nutritional status has passed
From deficiency to hunger
And from hunger to starvation,
But I have not known what it was that I lacked.

No one has really mastered me
Physically, intellectually and spiritually, all at once.
Many people have loved me
But they have either been overwhelmed
By something in their love for me so that they gave me
Only tenderness
Or they have been blind, insensitive, unknowledgeful
Of qualities I knew that I possessed
So that I could not take their brash conquest seriously

The woman in me craves to be mastered
Legitimately; because no one can pretend to conquest
Legitimately; from the cortex down,
Not by force alone
But by force as a concomitant mode of expression
Of intellectual dominance.

My Universe is boundless, but I want to find its limits
I want to find those limits in your arms
I want to try my hardest to get free . . . . . and fail

I want to cry out for mercy
But to find that you stop when it pleases you,
I want to discover that there are things I can't do
Ruses I can't get away with
Tricks I can't pull off
Because you can beat me at my own game, and outsmart me.
I want to fling myself to my limits
To the ends of my endurance and capacity
To the utmost corners of my devilment and imagination,
And still find myself held, loved and secure.

I want to ride out the fiercest storms
And buck the fiercest winds
Because my helm is in iron hands.

As a mare with pace and a velvet mouth
I want to feel the light hands of my rider
Gentle, but firm.

The next poem was written after several sessions in which the
poet had been concerned with the scrutiny of her own pattern of
behavior in psychosexual relationships. This introspective begin-
ning, however, is quickly dropped in favor of a more spontaneous
outburst which turns into a genuine paeon of praise for the happy
interchange of affection between the two individuals.

I am no strategist in love!
Having aroused your interest
I should now coyly retire,
Remaining inaccessible and faintly aloof.
My days should be heavily dated
My nights clearly filled
But diplomatically unspoken of.
I should never answer the phone
I should never write to you.

But what do I do?
Jam the mails with letters
Yelp with delight when you call
Drift through the days with a delirious expression
Of utter contentment,
And even answer your beck-and-or-call
To preposterous early morning dates,
Which ruin my sleep,
Not because I have no alarm clock
But because I'm just plain EXCITED.

EXCITED
        EXCITED
                EXCITED

Because I love to have you look at me
Man of distinction,

Because I love your twinkle, visual and verbal
Because I love it when you are just there
Though nothing is said or even thought of.

EXCITED
          EXCITED
                    EXCITED

Because I love your orderliness and proficiency,
Because I could sit for hours
Like a moonstruck adolescent
And watch you snap things into place.
Because, even in the anti-chamber of your working self
I catch a glimpse of the power I know and love
Efficiency, economy and ease.

EXCITED
          EXCITED
                    EXCITED

Because in your arms I can give you measure for measure
Because I have never known ecstasy without its counterpart of pain
Because I have never had pure undiluted joy.
Because I feel now, for the first time
That at long long last
This is what I was evolved for
(Among other things to be sure)
But this 'me'
This blend of mind and body
This particular combination of spirit and blood,
This particular constellation of molecules,
This 'me' has come a long way in space-time
To find just this mode of expression.
O darling, I crave joy like a drunkard
And you give it to me.

The next poem may be considered an epitome of a full realization of emotional potential. Unlike the little poem "When You Abandon Love" (see page 000) this catches an exultant mood.

Strong wine for your breakfast
Strong wine for your tea
Strong wine in a bedside cup—
And all that wine is me

Drink up your wine Darling
Drink all you can
The time in rocks
The time of clocks
Waits for no man

Drink all your wine Darling
It is your due
For I wouldn't be wine
Were it not for you

Drink up your wine Darling
Let your joy rise
Plant a kiss in the cup
Drink with lips and eyes

The poem entitled "Last Hour" is a recapitulation of many of the fundamental experiences in any therapeutic undertaking.

LAST HOUR

I awoke this morning
Having recaptured in sleep
The fragment of a prayer:
Said, conscientiously, as a child
Day by day
But long since forgotten, shelved, in disuse.
For the God of childhood
No longer demands of me
That I punch a prayerful time-clock
In order to register attendance
As a worshiper of love and beauty.

And the fragment runs:

That we may show forth praise
Not only with our lips

But in our lives;
By giving up ourselves to service.

And by walking in holiness and righteousness
All our days.

"That *we* may show forth praise,"—Who are *we?*
All those who have been privileged to struggle
Toward a fuller understanding,
All those who have been willing to recognize
The devious petty pilferings of parts of the self;
Those parts which competence, control and pride
So neatly cover.

All those who have demanded exposure
Of the falsehoods within,
Those falsehoods justified by reason and logic
And condoned by communal complacence.
We would show forth praise.

Praise? Yes, praise is important
For praise is jubilant and exultant.
Praise is energy cleanly channelled
With nothing lost from leakage or clogging.
Praise is carried in the clearest notes of the horn,
In the inspired and economic movements of the dance,
In the most exalted moments of love.
We would show forth *praise.*

Not only with our lips
But in our lives

How, with my lips,
Can I recapture—recapitulate—
All that has grown within me?
Hard, now, even to believe
That glimpse of an abyss—which brought me here.
Those moments when the ground was no longer solid,
Where hesitancy and doubt, like double images,
Confused the simplest choice or action.

Where fear had no focus,
And by this very feature
Turned to terror.
And from there?
To Hours when the couch appeared
As an exposed and isolated island;
No, as a little left-over fragment
In interstellar space
On which telescopes were trained
For scrutiny and censure.
And where silence seemed
A vast, impenitrable, secret, timeless condemnation.

And from there?
To Hours of establishing a new perspective.
Back on the sunny earth,
Warm and tangible.
Hours of disentangling the present from the past
The genuine from the counterfeit,
The life-giving from the life-destroying,
The facilitating from the hampering.

Hours when the distance between couch and chair
Was no longer measured in terms of light-years, miles,
        yards, feet,
For suddenly there was no longer emptiness and distance
There was communication in the very act of thinking.

And from there?

To Hours which passed as the sweep of the second hand
Across the face of the clock.
So crowded, so crammed, so chaotic the press of ideas
Which jostled each other for the chance of exposure
To objective scrutiny.
Hours when the pieces of an emotional puzzle,
Lay all assembled, but in disarray
Awaiting deft handling
To give them meaning and coherence.

And from there?

To Hours of acute longing
To be held only in a reassuring presence;
As by strong arms in night sickness.
To Hours of willingly accepted blindness
That one might know what it means to be led.
To Hours of dependency
That one might know what it means to trust implicitly,
To Hours of relinquishing even ones own identity
That one might know what it means to believe.

Not only with our lips
But in our lives.

These Hours are part of life, ingrained in me—
Only their shadows do my lips recapture.

By giving up ourselves to service

By giving up?
Yes, but not with resignation or with stifled bitterness;
Not in renunciation or from subservience or duty.
Rather with abandon and relaxation,
With concentration on the central values
And disregard of the peripheral.

By walking in holiness and righteousness all our days.

This may belong to an old idiom,
And the words may now be different
But not so the meaning:
To embody a new way of life at all levels,
At all times, and with all persons,
To make use of the linear coordinates
Of relentless honesty and love
In all complex human equations,
That have been learned
In the scrutiny of simpler actions.
To walk forward in faith with those who share
This core of experience—and to extend it to others.
For with this as a new birthright
I become heir to a goodly heritage.

The experience, evoked and expressed, of "becoming heir to a goodly heritage" seems a fitting closure to *The Therapy of Poetry*.

REFERENCES

1. Cane, Melville: *Making a Poem*. New York, Harcourt, Brace and Co., 1953.
2. Erikson, Erik H.: In Milton J. E. Senn (Ed.): *Symposium on the Healthy Personality*. Josiah Macy, Jr. Foundation, 1950.
3. Harrower, Molly: Child's call to arms. *London Graphic*, 1916.
4. Harrower, Molly: *Godolphin Bicentenary Play*. Salisbury, England, Bennett Bros., 1926.
5. Harrower, Molly: *Plain Jane*. New York, Coward-McCann, 1929.
6. Harrower, Molly: *Spiral and Other Poems*. El Paso, Ellis Bros., 1932.
7. Harrower, Molly: *Time to Squander, Time to Reap*. New Bedford, Reynolds DeWalt Printing, 1946 and 1965.
8. Harrower, Molly: Poems emerging from the therapeutic experience. *Journal of Nervous and Mental Disease, 149:*213–233, 1969.
9. Harrower, Molly: Autobiography. *Archives of the History of American Psychology*. Akron, Ohio: University of Akron, 1970.
10. Koffka, K.: *Principles of Gestalt Psychology*. New York, Harcourt, Brace, and Co., 1935.
11. Leedy, J. J. (Ed.): *Poetry Therapy*. Philadelphia, J. B. Lippincott Co., 1969.
12. Lerner, Arthur: *Psychoanalytically Oriented Criticism of Three American Poets: Poe, Whitman and Aiken*. Fairleigh Dickinson University Press, 1970.